D0984219

the Spirit of Gardening

Reflections on the true joys of gardening

by Jeff Cox

 Rodale Press, Emmaus, Pennsylvania

For Eric, Christopher, Shane, and Chandra

Illustrations by Frank Fretz
Book design by Linda Jacopetti

Library of Congress Cataloging-in-Publication Data

Cox, Jeff, 1940–
    The spirit of gardening.

    Includes index.
    1. Gardening. 2. Plants, Cultivated. I. Title.
SB455.3.C69   1986   635   86–13737
ISBN 0–87857–638–X hardcover

2 4 6 8 10 9 7 5 3 1 hardcover

Contents

The Earth that's Nature's mother is her tomb,
What is her burying grave, that is her womb,
And from her womb children of divers kind
We sucking on her natural bosom find,
Many for many virtues excellent,
None but for some and yet all different.
O mickle is the powerful grace that lies
In plants, herbs, stones and their true qualities,
For nought so vile that on the earth doth live
But to the earth some special good doth give.

—William Shakespeare
Romeo and Juliet
Act II, sc.2

Introduction

Our spirit shines into the world through the aperture of our awareness. The aperture opens as we grow and will continue to open throughout life, if we continue to grow in knowledge and wisdom. For that to happen, we must allow ourselves to change, for all growth is change.

Change doesn't have to be momentous to promote our spiritual growth. It can be simple, like switching from rows to raised beds in the garden or breaking a bad habit. But it must always be radical and strike to the core where our belief system lies. Rigid beliefs held in blind faith resist change. Learning becomes impossible. No growth occurs. But where new ideas are allowed to assault beliefs, truth is better served and our awareness is given a chance to expand.

As the aperture opens, it lets more of our spirit into the world—we become less vague, more real to those who know us. Conversely, we take in more of the world's spirit and see more deeply into it. We become more capable.

As yet, how much in life conspires to close down our awareness! Obsessive desires distract it. Dull routine shrivels it.

It seems that the real work of life is the fight to preserve and expand our awareness in the face of a constant entropic pressure to shut it down. If we win the fight, we grow. If we lose, our light becomes ever paler until, in some passionless moment that passes unrecognized, it disappears. The process is mirrored in the garden's imperative: grow or die.

Through the past sixteen circling seasons, I've
seen lots of personal, very human things reflected in
my garden, including awareness. Some kind of
awareness sends the root to water and turns a flower's face to the sun. Flowers are aware of something
when they devise ultraviolet markings to guide bees
to their nectaries, because bees can see in that part
of the spectrum. Trees in the forest become aware
that insects are attacking one of their number, and
all begin to manufacture repellent compounds in
their leaves.

Awareness, then, flows through all living things.
Being human, we're intimately familiar with the human expression of consciousness—so familiar that
we often fail to feel our connections to other living
beings. It's not hard to share a conscious moment
with a dog. It's less easy to feel the connection with a
pack of cawing crows. It takes an immense, open
detachment to connect our awareness to that of a
shrub.

Several times, however, I've shared a sense of
awareness with the plants around me in the garden.
Then I've known that life is a unified whole with
myriad eyes, two of which I was staring out of. My
life flowed together with all the lives around me, and
it was in this stream, by one of its quiet pools, that I
saw myself reflected.

I saw the wildness in me, and in the garden. I
understood that the urges and imperatives that
make a primeval forest are also at work in the bean
patch. If dog eats dog, then bug eats bug. Nature is
entirely present in each of her parts. We can thwart
her rules and break her rules, but we can't change
them. Neither can we wholly understand them. They
are an endless source of learning for us. No wonder
Thoreau said that in wildness is the preservation of
the world.

What's true for the individual is true for society. Civilizations are characterized by their belief systems, and when an old system is supplanted by a new one, an age passes. During the transition, moral codes thaw and change. Values are challenged. Meanings shift. People look for beliefs to share, but there is no consensus. We invent all manner of beliefs which, like our other purely human inventions, are dead—lifeless imitations of living processes. Our scientific knowledge runs far ahead of the ancient moral dogmas we've inherited.

To forge a better, more whole expression of human society, we must look to the root and core of our nature, where meaning is found. There we will find that our nature, like all nature, is essentially innocent. We have only to regain our innocence to find a social code adequate to our science.

I've learned much from plants that I feel is applicable to my inner life. These little enlargements of awareness have thrilled me. I get enthused and excited by my discoveries; this book is the result.

Enthusiasm and excitement are characteristic of all spirit: a spirited performance; the spirit that takes over a crowd at a big game; the spirit of gardening.

Spirit is the very animator of our lives, the deepest spark within us, the breath of life that blows the soil aflame and from its whirling energy produces both the garden and the gardener.

The plants are introduced as they broke through to my awareness while I was writing the book. I like to think that the order of presentation, as well as the content of the essays, is the plants' contribution.   Jeff Cox
                                                   February 27, 1986

Pachysandra

*T*he deep frosts of winter freeze our patch of evergreen pachysandra to a dull, dingy green, but as the sun gets a little stronger, before the robins return or the buds burst or the snow is entirely melted, the pachysandra freshens up, the very first sign of spring.

This year I noticed how it has grown a bit from the previous year. Each year it shows increase.

The patch started small, just a handful of leafy stalks with moist roots given to Marilyn by her dad twelve years ago. She found the perfect location for this low ground cover—in a moist, shady, humusy, woodsy spot along the path to the springhouse. It has since naturalized to a circular patch 15 feet across, extending its diameter about a foot a year. This is small progress, but it's thorough. Pachysandra colonizes the soil so thickly with its stoloniferous roots that few weeds can compete with it.

Like a solid investment, its growth is slow, sure, and steady. When the pachysandra was young, I might have sown a few dollars in blue chip investments. You turn around, and it's ten years later, and the nest egg has doubled. But we spent our money on things like fruit trees, crosscut hand pruners, shrubs, perennial flowers, and more pachysandra instead. Around here, the horticulture priority is a high one.

Pachysandra is a low-risk crop: It's extremely hardy, and if it likes its spot, it will slowly expand its turf without much help from us. Were it to be lost to drought or the tracks of a backhoe, that would be no great loss. Pachysandra keeps a low profile in every situation. Low work. Low risk. Low yield.

Corn, by contrast, is a high-risk, high-work cash crop with a lot riding on it. It needs reseeding every year. Drought can stunt it. Smut can smite it. But a bagful of seed can fill a barn. High work. High risk. High yield.

My investments, now that I look back, were paid for in hard currency—sweat and cash. Their dividends are more ethereal: the perfume of the mock orange in the noontime air, the glimpse of a brazen robin cheerily robbing my cherries. Perhaps I'm paid off in the taste of a berry. Or the whiff of the breath from the soft, sweet earth on a sunny spring morning.

I like the way pachysandra pays me back, in little increments of money-green leaves. It shows me that the little progresses are important. While I busied myself with other things, the pachysandra grew. Now all the land is locked in the drab, ruined colors of late winter. The pachysandra, plumped out in its new fresh green, suggests the deluge of plants to come. For the little work this plant requires, a first hello from nature is handsome payment indeed.

Japanese
Plums

*T*he most fearsome sound I ever heard was the crash made by our ancient, hollow-trunked apple tree when it fell during a monstrous ice storm. I'd seen an ice storm that bad only once before, when I was a kid, and this time I remembered with a shock the sound of tree limbs all over the forest cracking and falling off under the weight of tons of coating ice. These cracking, crashing sounds had been going on for hours, keeping me awake and fretful, when I heard a roar and a thunderous crack, like lightning striking, followed by a crash so loud I jumped away from the window, expecting the house to fall apart. The old apple—a huge tree of immense girth—was down.

Eventually, of course, the sky cleared and the chain saws removed the wreckage, revealing a bald spot on the slope left by the vanished tree. The warming sun would soon call forth long-dormant briars, brambles, and weeds. I was looking for something to plant there when a friend offered me some Japanese plums. I knew nothing about them, but took two and placed them 20 feet apart, flanking the severed stump of the apple.

Given the rich duff of decayed generations of apples, a southwest view, and plenty of water, the trees flourished. Now eight years old, the pair of them are the stars of that part of the property.

The far tree grew into a narrow vase shape, 40 feet tall but hardly 10 feet in diameter. The near tree is just as big, but horizontal. It spreads 30 feet wide but no more than 15 feet tall. Now, in the early springtime, both are flocked with white blossoms, the far tree *en pointe*, and the near tree low and arched backwards.

The tall, skinny one produces cherry red plums the size of Ping-Pong balls that hang like ornaments along the upright limbs. They are the sweetest and tangiest of the two trees' fruit, but they're out of my reach.

The short, wide tree makes big, goose-egg-shaped plums with a waxy feel to their purplish skin. The taste is rather attenuated and carries a strange tone that I don't like. But they are always right there, hanging within reach.

It's as if these two trees agreed to divvy up qualities—one has good fruit in a bad position, the other has bad fruit in a good position.

Despite this little joke, the two have filled the space where the old apple had been with a *pas-de-deux* of graceful energy. I noticed this year that the limbs of the tall tree spiraled to the left to touch the shorter one, which spirals to the right to reach around the taller one. Together they swirl around the spot where the apple tree had been, flanking its rotted stump, which is now memorialized by a spray of cinnamon ferns.

While the plums have made the spot their own, their shapes pay homage to the ancient apple that preceded them, allowing the past into the present without compromising either.

From the way they're growing, I'd say those trees will remember the old apple for as long as they stand in their complementary arrangement. I can see the big apple in my mind's eye, extending up through the empty vortex between the plums. No one else could know of this imaginary apple tree. But then, unless one knows the parent, it's hard to see her in the daughter, or the father in the son.

*Dutchman's
Breeches*

*I*n *Little Friends from Holland,* a picture book I had as a child, there recurred the image of a stout Dutch peasant of the early nineteenth century, smoking a pipe, his baggy white trousers tied at the waist with a sash and pegged at the ankles just above his wooden shoes.

Is it mere nostalgia that invests childhood memories with such power later in life, or is it that they are the mental seeds around which our world view once crystallized?

Whatever it is, it became operational when Marilyn first showed me the picture of dutchman's breeches, *Dicentra cucullaria,* in a book of American wild flowers. For some reason, the plant was extraordinarily intriguing. I wanted it in our garden. I was to wait a long time.

As the years passed, we acquired several of its cousins. First we planted bleeding heart, *Dicentra spectabilis,* below a shelf of large rocks in our shade garden. It's an early spring riser that hangs out its floral valentines in mid-April.

We also discovered and planted an everblooming type, *Dicentra formosa,* with less spectacular

flowers, a little farther down the side of the shelf of
rocks. We made a mental note to add *Dicentra
eximia*, fringed bleeding heart, to this group. By that
time, we'd forgotten about the dutchman's
breeches, the wild member of the genus.

On a mid-April day last year, we took a scenic
drive along the road that hugs the west bank of the
Delaware River near Philadelphia. The road is narrow, rustic, shady, and is built against steep shale
and slate cliffs that descend to the river, overhung
with huge, ancient trees. As we drove along, I noticed masses of small white flowers on fluffy-looking
grey-green foliage growing on ledges on the rock
cliffs, but I couldn't recognize them as we blurred
past at 40 miles per hour. After a bit, we turned off
the river road and struck off up a steep lane that we
knew would lead us home.

Thirty yards up this side road, I saw the white
flowers again and stopped the car to see what they
were. As we approached them, we both said the
name at once: "dutchman's breeches."

We carefully dug a small clump from an extensive patch lining the roadside, rolled it gently in a
paper bag, and wet it down with water from a nearby
stream.

When we arrived home an hour later, Marilyn
knew just where to put the plants—on a ledge filled
with soil above the shelf of rock that was bordered
by the other dicentras. This ledge, in turn, was sheltered by a taller outcropping of rock.

We planted the dutchman's breeches and kept

it watered, but the foliage withered and died by mid-May. We had no idea whether it would return this spring. In fact, I'd pretty much forgotten about it when, on a balmy April evening this year, hauling kitchen scraps to the compost pile, I noticed a large mass of feathery, ferny foliage by the big rock in the shade garden. It was the dutchman's breeches, already beginning to hang out its white wash.

Not only had it survived, but it had tripled in size and was flourishing. I realized that the spot Marilyn had given it was craftily chosen—perched above its cultivated cousins on a shady, rocky ledge much like its original home.

If we'd planted it in rich soil, with unfamiliar neighbors, in the sun of one of our regular perennial beds, it probably would have sulked and died out. One plant's ideal conditions are another plant's burial ground.

It's the same with people. When I've done jobs I didn't like, I've always had the same reaction: a feeling of suffocation. But plant me behind my relic of a typewriter or in front of my drawing board and I flourish. Someone else, perhaps, would not like to confront the blank piece of paper each morning.

A person who loves his or her work is like a plant in the right spot—there, growth is maximized and yield is greatest.

Virginia Bluebells

*W*hen we first encounter other living beings, whether human, plant, or animal, we get a superficial impression such as the eyes give: all surfaces and gross boundaries. But each being goes much deeper, its personality suggested by its shape or movements, or in the case of humankind, by speech. This personal glow emanates from each creature. We feel it rather than see it. Either we like it or we don't, and our response is determined by the feel of the quality of the personality.

It's this feeling process that's at the root of our ability to penetrate the surfaces and boundaries of other creatures and begin to explore their richness. Initially, we're like blind persons in strange rooms. We must feel our way through the new twists and turns, discover things familiar and unfamiliar, in order to flesh out an honest inner image of what that personality is like. I say honest because many times our inner images are partially self-created: Our expectations and prejudices distort the true image we'd get from a dispassionate appraisal. Such dislocations of reality are dangerous precipices, over which we slip into hurt, anger, and grief when what we expect is confounded.

My first awareness of Virginia bluebells (*Mertensia virginica*) dawned as Marilyn and I drove through a dappled young forest at the end of an

April day over a decade ago. The forest floor was
spotted with clumps of 2-foot plants with blue flowers—a light cerulean blue that I particularly like. I
asked her what they were.

"Virginia bluebells," she told me, and we
agreed that we'd love to grow some in our woods.

Years passed before we brought home a clump
from Marilyn's grandmother's woodsy bank of
perennials. They had just finished flowering and
were declining. A few straggly bells hung under the
topmost leaves, but the plants looked weak and flac-
cid. Before May was finished, their tops had died
back to the ground.

Early the next spring, I hunted under the leaf
litter to see if they were emerging. Some small, soft,
dusty green leaves and fleshy stems with very shal-
low roots came up in my hand. I was digging up the
bed of seedling bluebells! Tucking the seedlings'
roots back into the soil, I pushed some litter back
over them and left nature to take its course.

I came to understand something about the bluebells. They were very soft and delicate plants, obviously self-sowers, as the just-sprouted seedlings con-
firmed.

In a few weeks, full-blown plants had shot up to
18 inches and were getting ready to flower. Their
leaves hung pale and rather limp to the touch—but
now I knew that this was their habit, not the consequence of a hard environment. The flower buds
emerged everywhere from the leaf axils—surprisingly pink. Had we brought home a pink cultivar? I
was disappointed, for it was their blue that I loved.

A day or two later, the pink buds opened into the glowing true-blue bells that I wanted. Each bell-shaped flower is formed from a single piece of luminous, blue tissue, scalloped daintily along the lip of the bell, with five gold-tipped stamens for clappers.

As many gardeners do with a new flower, I bent down to smell a bunch. A light, sweet, clean scent freshened my nose.

After flowering, the plants died back quickly. They make an early appearance, play their visual music during late April and early May, and then fall back to sleep until the next spring. Mertensia prefers the moist and humusy woods' edge or shaded spot. It could never stand the rugged sun of August or the parched soil of September. Nor would its note of true blue be appropriate in the summer. It belongs with the robin's eggs and the spring skies. When it's showery, flowery, and bowery, mertensia is happy.

I think of all the people I meet and how rich in experience and personality attributes they must be. There's no time to get to know everyone the way I've learned to know the Virginia bluebell. But to sense the river of life running under every skin is to give people their worth, for the river is deep and inestimable.

The natural impulse that resulted in mertensia finds expression somewhere within me, too. It's one of my best places.

Filberts

*T*hree kinds of filberts grow on my property. One is all business. The second is a creative artist. The third is the wild Bohemian of the group—beyond my command.

The businessmen are hybrid, nut-bearing, woody bushes with many stems planted in a group of three, making a triangle of space that contains a large rock. I have to use a stepladder to reach the nuts on the outside of the triangle, but the rock gives me a place to stand in the shrubs' enclosure to reach high on the inner limbs for the choicest nuts. The three bushes give us about a gallon of husked nuts each fall, which we cure and freeze. They last us until next nut season.

Our nut-bearing filberts are hybrids of *Corylus avellana*, the European filbert, and several native American species. Genes of *Corylus maxima*, which gives outsized nuts, also lurk in these shrubs.

Having been many years in the nut business and not concerned with appearance, the filbert bushes are ordinary looking. They form a dense, green backdrop for the tiered garden of perennial flowers that spills down the slope toward the house. They are early to work, hanging out 2-inch, dusty yellow catkins in late winter. It's too cold at that time of year for big, delicate flowers, so the bushes, which carry male and female parts on the same branches, have devised a foul-weather flower. Several tiny, thread-thin red wands poke through a minuscule opening at the center of a female bud to collect pollen and guide it to the ovary deep within the bud.

Summer finds the bushes humming away, ripening their nuts. By September, when thumb pressure easily loosens the nuts from their receptacles in the husks and the husks themselves are browning in the sun, the nuts are ready to pick. The filberts always seem relieved after harvest, shaken out and picked over, and they finish the season in a slow, browning decline, obviously enjoying their do-nothing retirement.

Harry Lauder's walking stick is the artist of the group. Its botanical name is *Corylus avellana* 'Contorta,' which means it's the contorted version of European filbert, or hazel as it's called in England. This twisty sport of *C. avellana* was found growing wild in England.

If you follow along the length of a limb, you immediately see its unpredictability. It will grow in one direction for a few inches and then suddenly take off at a randomly chosen angle. In full leaf, the winding twists and turns of its branches are hard to see. But in the leafless winter, against white snow, Contorta becomes a most entertaining creature, like its common namesake, Harry Lauder. Lauder was born in 1870 and died in 1950. He was the darling of the English music hall circuit in turn-of-the-century London, singing comic songs at first, but then turning to sentimental songs like "Roamin' in the Gloamin'" and "I Love a Lassie."

Lauder was the archetypal Scotsman in the kilt, with a gnarled, twisted walking stick, singing his heart out about the bonnie braes. In fact, Lauder's actual walking stick was most likely filbert and very possibly *Corylus avellana* 'Contorta.' Hazel was often used for tool handles and walking sticks in Europe at that time.

The artist may be unpredictable, but he's nevertheless in the garden, performing for the public, which is more than one can say for *Corylus americana*, the wild filbert that grows along the unkempt woods' edge at the southern end of our property. Its nuts are small and intensely flavored. It grows where it pleases and doesn't mix with the cultivated society of its cousins within my gardens. Like any true Bohemian, the wild filbert heeds its own inner call and offers little to people except its presence.

I spy these three types in human society, too, and it takes all of them to make society work. The business people ensure profits for themselves and for the creative artists who conceive and design products. The Bohemian life is an escape valve, a place where the wild nuts grow.

And so my property is replete with a society of hazelnuts. They feed me. They amuse me. They sound nature's wild note. And on a deeper level, as the ancient druids of Ireland knew, they are one of the most mystical of trees. I find myself enjoying their company quite often. I go to them through a secret affinity described best by William Butler Yeats, when he wrote, "I went down to the hazel wood, because a fire was in my head."

Mullein

*I*n Colonial America, ships going from England to Norfolk carried tea, finished goods, passengers, and soil shoveled into the hold as ballast. It was in such ballast, dumped on Virginia's shores, that mullein (*Verbascum thapsus*) came to America, spreading across the continent until today it's found from Alaska's North Slope to southern Mexico, from Labrador to Key West. Last year it was also found sprouting from the face of a dry wall I'd built to create a terrace for low-growing perennial flowers.

Mullein in its first year makes a large rosette of grey-green leaves with the texture of sheared wool or good flannel. The leaves are large and inviting to the touch. The plant is doing most of its first-year work in secret, forming the large root that will hold the resources for flowering in the second season.

The mullein in my stone wall emerged facing outward into the yard rather than up toward the sun, like a grey-green medallion affixed to the wall, nature's prize ribbon bestowed on the garden by a deva.

I anticipated the second year of this biennial's life. Would its tall flower stalk curve out and upward when it appeared from the wall? Or would it stick out into the yard, ribbon become lance, to joust with passing lawn mowers and young fielders drifting back for high-fly Whiffle Balls?

An odd seed of the plant must have germinated in the disturbed soil behind two layers of rock. Such will to live accounts for the plant's enormous range.

Mullein leaves are surprisingly soft and warm. Last summer I knelt by the wall and stroked the plant's leaves. They felt good. The sun and the quietness of the moment carried me back to a faraway summer when the slogan was, "If it feels good, do it!" I remember what a sacred expression it was, and how many people felt threatened by it. Someone would always say, "If it feels good for me to go out in the street and shoot someone, should I do it?" Someone would always answer, "Is that what you would do if there was no one to stop you?"

Those who accepted that slogan decided that new rules were needed, rules built closer to the fundamentals of human nature. All the old rules were inspected for utility and discarded if they seemed irrelevant or repressive. Old moral systems seemed like isolated ships in which closed-minded groups sailed through life. But many people in those days jumped overboard and found themselves in an ocean of uncertainty. Some of these panicked. Others were eaten by sharks. Those who clung to the Golden Rule best weathered the storms: They had a direction, at least, toward a kinder place.

"If it feels good, do it!" meant to look at one's own feelings for the answers to moral questions, not to hand-me-down religions. It meant to trust one's inherent goodness.

The phrase threatened people because it called them to leap from their boats and swim, perhaps drown. Their clerics and their mores had always defined what was right and wrong, not their own hearts. "If it feels good . . . " threatened because such license, in the wrong hands, could lead to wantonness and mayhem, openly perpetrated. But the individual heart is also the repository of goodness, and such a heart can be trusted.

Thus people's hearts are tested. Those that contain a living germ of life, like good seed, will grow.

I waited for the mullein to reappear from the wall and make a flower stalk, but its root must have dried out over the winter. It didn't come back. I missed seeing its tall spike dotted with pale yellow flowers like moths settled on it to sip nectar.

Yet I don't lack for mullein. Several flower stalks appeared along the fencerow at the back of the property, choosing the roughest places to do the other imperative of those strange days almost two decades ago: their own thing.

Onions

*W*e could fairly rename this country The Onionited States of America, so thoroughly do onions inhabit every part of it. Wild garlic (*Allium canadense*) grows everywhere on my land. In late April, its masses of blue-green spears are set against forest green ground covers like *Vinca minor*, and contrast with the light, yellow-green foliage of emergent weeds. The effect is one we strive to create in the garden, usually with less success.

Wild garlic dominates the American landscape right through the Midwest. Chicago was the Indian name for "place of the wild onion." The wild onion, properly, is *Allium drummondii*, found in the Plains states and Rocky Mountains. A prairie onion, *Allium stellatum*, grows in the High Plains only. Which species sustained Lewis and Clark when they had no other food on their trek west, we don't know, but they claimed "wild onions" saved them from starvation.

My garden is also suffused with onions. We use the culinary kind to edge our raised beds, hoping to mask the scent of tender broccoli and lettuce within the onions' picket lines and protect them from marauding insects.

Our perennial flower gardens contain several kinds of chives, another branch of the Allium tribe. And one of the most spectacular flowers of all is *Allium giganteum*, the big ornamental onion that bursts open with 4-inch purple balls atop tall, blue-green wands in summer.

Onions aren't bothered by bugs and they don't take much work, although the edible kinds make bigger bulbs if the flowering stems are pulled off as they appear. Onions give reproduction a high priority. If that option is kept closed, they tend to get fat, and fat onions are what we want.

We braid the onions when they're ripe and hang the braids from a pole slung between beams up in the cool sleeping loft. They last until March. Good keeping onions, like the Northern Oak variety we buy from the Stokes catalog, tend to be no-nonsense onions. They make me cry bitterly, to the point where I drop the knife and run in real pain for the soothing water of the sink tap.

The cut bulbs exude a sulfur-laden gas that turns to sulfuric acid when it hits anything wet, including the moisture that coats the eyeballs. Rinsing the eyes with plain water works because it dilutes the acid and rinses it away.

Onions reach out in other ways to remind us of their presence. Cows that graze spring pastures can give milk with an unpleasant garlic flavor imparted by *Allium canadense* in the browse, although I haven't tasted garlic milk in years. Thank goodness.

Onions seem to be responsible for keeping sulfur moving in the soil's nutrient cycles. I suppose that all the plants together keep all the elements moving, turning into tissue, becoming sugar, spilling at death into the soil, there to be taken up by fungi and other decomposers, who die in their turn, spilling the same elements back into the soil in combinations now suited to the nutrition of plants.

The elements spin in the wheel, alive, then dead, then alive again. Are they really ever dead, or just quiescently waiting to be hoisted aloft aboard another green tower? The elements in my body—are "my" atoms alive? My atoms certainly have hooked together to make up my physical being, and so share in my life.

The onion and I boil up out of the same atomic soup. We share the same world. Perhaps I eat the onion. Then some of its elements become a part of me. Some day, perhaps, wild garlic will find nourishment in my ashes. These onions and I, we share the very substance of life itself.

Onions grow in layers that emerge one by one from a basal growing point. Try to find the growing point itself and it recedes one more layer beneath your reach. Although it's vanishingly small, it remains the point of potency. It is not a thing as much as a spirit. If I look inside myself, I see that there's also a place from which all else emerges, a similar point of potency. Layers of experience and tough skins protect that place.

Onions are ripe when their tops fall over and begin to dry. My favorite garden task is pulling ripe onions. They all come up grinning from ear to ear. What a time they must have had in these fine raised beds, triple-dug and laced with rotting manures, watered during dry spells. I lay them out in neat lines on the flagstone path to cure.

I figure life's worth living if I can make just one onion happy.

Goldenseal

*W*e have a remarkable friend, a man in his sixties, who knows where the ginseng, goldenseal, and other rare herbs grow in the forests and fields of Berks County, Pennsylvania. Not only does he have a mental map of patches of herbs that he's found or been shown before, but he has a sixth sense about where to find new ones.

One drizzly spring day we were driving with Mountain Bummy, as he styles himself, when he pulled the car over, looked into the woods, and said, "You'll find ginseng in there." Marilyn and I looked around in the woods but we couldn't see any of the five-leaved shapes that fit our mental image of ginseng. Bummy found some right away.

He once showed us a patch of goldenseal (*Hydrastis canadensis*) that filled the forest floor beneath a stand of maples. The plants grow about 18 inches tall on herbaceous, hairy stems. Each stem divides near the top, and its branches end in hairy leaves with five or seven deeply divided lobes. In spring the plant carries a frothy-looking, creamy flower, and in late summer, a cluster of red berries appears. Ginseng also has red berries in late summer. But then so do jack-in-the-pulpit and several other nonwoody plants of the forest floor.

Years ago we transplanted a few roots of golden-seal from a huge patch Bummy had shown us and put them with some ginseng seedlings we'd started in our woods. Today the goldenseal patch is about 3 by 5 feet and the ginseng brings a root or two to maturity for us each year. I collect and plant the berries of both goldenseal and ginseng in the area around the existing patches to keep them growing and rejuvenated.

Both plants prefer rich, stony soil and a woodsy, out-of-the-way spot in the shade. We've given them a place protected by blackberries, already inhabited by *Vinca minor*, pink lady's slipper, wild ginger, and mountain laurel.

These are our heavy-duty healing plants, especially the goldenseal. It has fleshy roots that dry thin and hard to a greenish yellow color. Marilyn whizzes them in a blender until they turn to powder, and sometimes we powder them in a large mortar and pestle.

The powder makes tincture and salve. The tincture is made with a couple of ounces of goldenseal powder, a similar amount of powdered myrrh, and a half-ounce of crushed red cayenne pepper steeped at room temperature in a half gallon of ethyl alcohol, which can be purchased at liquor stores as neutral grain spirits of 180 proof. This tincture is not for internal use. We shake up the half gallon jar every few days for a few weeks, then pour off the liquid from the leached residues of the powders. This concoction is our remedy for cuts, scratches, or any other tear or sore on the skin. It burns like crazy on a fresh cut, but it makes us feel secure that the cut is not going to get infected.

The salve is made with 2 parts goldenseal powder and 1 part myrrh dissolved in warmed olive oil. We let this mixture sit for a couple of weeks so that all the medicinal properties of the powders are leached into the oil. Marilyn then strains off the oil and mixes it with enough melted beeswax to make the mixture solid when cool, but soft to the touch, and easily melted by skin temperature.

We use the salve for burns and abrasions, especially on kids who fall off bicycles. The salve keeps the skin medicated and soft so that it doesn't form hard scabs that pinch when an elbow or knee is bent.

We first made tincture and salve at a previous residence, where I had to tend two coal stoves over a long winter. I'd burned and scraped my left hand on one of the stoves, and the thing wouldn't heal. Marilyn tried healing notions from the drugstore, but they didn't work. So she consulted *Back to Eden*, a book by herbalist Jethro Kloss, who praised the virtues of goldenseal in tincture and salve. The salve healed that scrape within a few days, and from then on, it raised our children.

Ginseng, on the other hand, is a tonic in a different way. I like to eat the fresh roots, pulled from the ground in September after the berries ripen, scrubbed, and sliced into spicy wafers. I trust that ginseng has virtues that are not immediately apparent the way goldenseal's are. Somehow I feel mentally refreshed after eating a ginseng root each year.

Goldenseal heals my body and ginseng heals some other part of me, more internal and subjective.

Cherries

*T*he names of cherry varieties are as sweet and rich and red as the fruit: Biggareau, Black Tartarian, Emperor Francis. When I moved to this place, I pored over catalogs and ran the cherries through my fancy like rubies through my fingers. I liked the whole idea of cherries—dark drops of sugar under the green leaves, filling my bowl.

I chose a Black Tartarian and an Emperor Francis for the orchard which was then just taking shape in the upper field. When the trees were two years old, we felled a large poplar growing at the west end of the orchard that threw too much shade. It landed squarely on the Black Tartarian, smashing it to the roots. The next spring I replanted with another Black Tartarian. Although the Emperor Francis had a three-year head start, after a decade the Black Tartarian is twice the size of the older tree.

My visions of the trees loaded with cherries treaded water in my mind for several years while the orchard grew to maturity. Blossoms were sparse in those first years, and once a frost destroyed the whole crop. After about five years, the trees produced enough fruit to fill a bowl, but the birds ate it or ruined it all. Robins are the worst culprits, slashing the fruit with their beaks and pecking holes in every cherry.

I was reduced to nibbling carefully at the little good parts between slashes and holes. Occasionally, under the good part would be a worm. What a treat for the birds. First they enjoyed the sweet flesh of the cherry, then found the worm for dessert.

But there was not much of a treat for me. The trees were almost mature and bearing well, but edible cherries were as scarce as ever.

Growing the trees was obviously only half the task. Bringing in a crop would require carefully timed controls for the worms, which are the larvae of a fly or moth that lays its eggs on the young fruit. I'd have to find out the name of the pest and when it emerges. The birds would have to be kept off the trees with bird netting, or kept away by other means.

An inflatable plastic snake didn't work. The birds went straight past it to slash and hack the cherries. I priced bird netting. You could buy crates of cherries for what it would cost to protect a pailful. Not far from here is a large commercial orchard that used to have two anti-bird devices: One fired blank shotgun shells every three minutes and another emitted a horrible honk in counterpoint. The birds ate the orchardist's cherries anyway.

There are a dozen mature Bing cherry trees on an old farmstead within two miles of that commercial orchard. Once we saw these trees hanging heavy with fruit—clusters of five or more large, perfectly ripe Bings covering each limb tip, weighting them down within reach. Mysteriously, no birds had found the fruit—they were all at the commercial orchard playing cops and robbers with the orchardist.

Marilyn and I figured those old trees had decided that enough was enough, that they'd given decades of shy crops and bird-bitten crops, and now they would produce a crop for people.

Now I understood how to live with the cherries in my own orchard. Unless I wanted to get into annual tree covering and moth spraying, I would have to wait on the cherries themselves. Thirty, maybe fifty years from now, my trees, too, would drip with a bonanza of fruit. The birds would understand and stay away. Marilyn and I would totter out there and be enormously grateful for the once-in-a-lifetime harvest.

I had to learn to be an orchardist without expectations, at the very least. Cherry trees are strong-willed creatures, like horses at pasture, so I decided to let them have their head.

Since making this decision a few years ago, I've been satisfied each year to nibble carefully around the pecked-out parts, just as before, but now each cherry is half there instead of half gone. I see what I'm getting instead of what I'm missing. The little tastes keep my hopes up for the bonanza I know is sure to come.

Grapes

A grape seed sprouts and sends up one leafy shoot in its first year. Where the leaves attach to the shoot, new buds form over the summer. In the autumn, the leaves drop off and the mature buds are seen to be tucked against the cane, ready for rigorous winter.

The next spring, last year's initial shoot becomes one-year-old wood, brown and grooved, but not yet covered with bark. The buds swell in the warm spring. Each bud produces a fresh shoot arrayed with leaves and, perhaps, some fruit. While the leaves soak up the summer sun and the fruit ripens, buds again form in the leaf axils. In autumn the fruit is harvested and the leaves fall, revealing the new buds.

The next spring, that initial shoot has become a two-year-old trunk bearing several canes. Each bud on every cane will produce a shoot with leaves and possibly fruit.

And so on, *ad infinitum*.

You can see how the grapevine remains forever young: A shoot fruits once, then becomes scaffolding for succeeding years' shoots. The number of buds multiplies geometrically: If each shoot carries 10 buds, and each of those buds eventually grows into a shoot with 10 buds, after a few years a vine will have 10,000 buds.

And it would, except that as it extends itself without pruning, it loses vigor. The more buds on the vine, past an optimum carrying capacity, the weaker the new shoots become, and the fewer buds are made for the next season. Thus the vine races passionately for maximum growth, entwining its lover's arms around trees or posts, until exhaustion cools its ardor.

How passionately it produces fruit, too. Not as a single berry here or there, or even a cluster of five, but cascades of berries, rich with flavor, that will become one-third sugar before they raisin away.

The yeast that grows patiently on the grape skins all summer passionately attacks the sugar when the grape finally bursts. I've seen vats of wine boiling with bubbles of carbon dioxide given off by the wildly multiplying yeast.

After this mad embrace, the yeast and grape are gone, and wine remains. Humans have long known that the echo of this passion remains in the wine, a cheerful genie that will lead the unwary or intemperate into a swirling stupor.

More than most other plants, grapevines cling tenaciously to life, heat and drought only sweetening the berries and concentrating their flavors.

Vineyardists rein in this wild plant, forcing it to a more sociable size with heavy pruning, leaving it a paltry sixty buds out of its crazy potential for millions. The vine, to compensate, responds with more powerful growth, producing large shoots and bigger bunches of grapes. It makes its very best fruit in the most northerly part of its range, where the living isn't necessarily easy. "To make great grapes, vines have to suffer, rather like athletes," one fellow vineyardist told me.

Though the vine will never escape the bonds the vineyardist sets on it, it will keep trying. And in the trying it will triumph.

The grape's story sounds almost human: growing wildly and passionately in youth, discovering natural limits to the expenditure of such passion, finding that perhaps some further self-imposed limits serve to discipline and invigorate it. Then flourishing within those limits, the fruit of its work only better for the hardships endured.

Columbines

$\mathcal{F}$ollowing nature's imperative to cover the land and shade the soil, broad-leaved plants evolved to intercept as much sunlight, and thereby shade as much soil, as possible. Where their large flat leaves don't quite touch, thin shafts of sunlight penetrate to the soil below, creating an opportunity for a plant to take advantage of that unused energy.

So grass evolved. Its leaves are long and thin, like the shafts of light they were designed to intercept.

Thus form follows function in living things. The platypus has a duck's bill because that shape is best suited to its function of tearing weeds off the bottom of a pond. The functions of plants and animals can be intertwined so thoroughly that the creatures become quite dependent on one another—like the farmer ants and the unique fungus that only grows in the ants' burrows, and on which the ants totally subsist. Such interdependent creatures' forms are often complementary, related in appearance because they are related in function.

Which brings us to the long nectaries of the columbines, those graceful spurs that flare from the back of the flower and give it a flying, birdlike appearance.

To get to the drop of nectar at the end of the spurs, pollinators must brush past an array of pollen-covered anthers. As they withdraw, pollen is scattered over the pistil, fertilizing a plentiful load of seeds.

Species with extra long spurs are pollinated by hummingbirds or certain types of long-tongued moths. In fact, spurs resemble the shape of a hummingbird's beak, and the beak fits the spur like a hand fits a glove. These flowers usually carry five spurs clustered around a central tower of yellow anthers. If you look at the flower full in the face, you can see down into the bluish recesses of its nectaries—places that the moths and hummingbirds know so well, but that remain unknown to most humans. What delicious, clean food nectar is, served in a glowing, blue cup!

Species with shorter spurs have a different set of pollinators, including bumblebees, other moths, and smaller bees. One of the short-spur kind is *Aquilegia canadensis*, the little red and yellow wild columbine found east of the Rockies. Each flower has four, rather than five, spurs, and these are less than an inch long. The plant maintains its species integrity in the wild because it has a set of pollinators entirely different than *Aquilegia longissima*, an extremely long-spurred species (up to 8 inches), or *Aquilegia caerulea*, a pretty blue species, both of which share with *A. canadensis* its range along the Rocky Mountains' spine.

The columbines most of us grow in our gardens are hybrids of all these wild species, selected for color and graceful, long spurs.

For years I've admired columbines, but never more than after I learned about the form and functions of their spurs. Sitting recently with a small stand of *Aquilegia canadensis*, which we've tucked along the path in our terraced perennial garden, I realized that all the shapes of all the plants around me reflect their functions, not just the spurs of the columbines. All creatures, in fact, look the way they do in response to their strategy for living. Change the strategy and the form will change.

I've seen it happen in people. I knew a fellow who was a self-centered, ambitious, and rather unhappy young man. In his late twenties he underwent a change of strategy—an epiphany, one could say—where he took his eyes off himself and turned them on the world. There he saw pain to be alleviated, problems to be solved, people who needed someone to care. His face changed. With his new attitude, he really looked different, and the change was all for the better.

I would like to be able to read all the functions represented in natural forms the way I can see the story of the hummingbird's beak and tongue in the columbine's spur. I'd like to know which came first and who's manipulating who. I look at myself and again see form following function. Even inwardly, as I visit the chambers of my mind, reaching deep inside them for some insight, I am able to reach that nectar only if I can fit my understanding to the concept.

Morel Mushrooms

J don't grow morel mushrooms. I find them, if I'm lucky. Their botanical name, *Morchella esculenta*, means esculent morel, and lightly sautéed in a little butter, they are meaty, earthy, and altogether a more delicious edible than anything I cultivate on the property.

They appear in early to mid-May, on sunny days after a rain and a cool night. They prefer old orchards where ancient apple trees are moldering away, although they'll grow on other decaying wood too. For three or four years after our old apple fell in the big ice storm, morels appeared in a circle where its roots were decaying. The morel we pick and eat is the fruiting body of the morel fungus, and it's this fungus that helps pull the old apple wood apart. Under the soil, colonizing the dead roots, the hyphae of the fungus spread out, flourish, produce their several seasons of morels, then die away. I haven't found any morels there for the past two years.

Fungi like morels work on the downside of the cycle of growth, death, and decay, pulling dead organic matter apart into its constituents, which can then be used by other creatures to build new plant and animal structures. Fungi do this work in secret, ordinarily, down under the leaf litter on the forest floor, or in last year's rotting stalks that thatch the meadow soil under this year's new green tops.

They don't always work on dead wood. Mycorrhizal fungi live off the nourishing substances exuded by host plants' roots. These fungi sheathe the roots, and their structures spread out many feet into the soil beyond the roots. There they do something very strange, for a supposedly unsophisticated plant like a fungus. They absorb phosphorus compounds from the soil and pump them back to the plant roots, which pull them into the plant to build healthy tissue. For the plant, the effect is like having a much greater area of nutrient-absorbing feeder roots. In return, the plant manufactures the root exudate that the fungus favors. It must cost the plant less energy to make the root exudate than to grow more extensive feeder roots. The fungus, on the other hand, gets to lap up its favorite food and repays the plant with phosphorus and other nutrients.

Both plant and fungus win. Cooperation benefits both.

I'm tempted to say that competition, conversely, benefits only the victor. But in nature, competition may be only cooperation in disguise. For example, consider the wolves and caribou. Their relationship would seem a fierce competition to the death. But the wolves cull the weak and sick animals first, because they're easily caught. This "cleans" the herd, preventing the spread of whatever disease afflicted the caribou taken by the wolves. The herd loses an individual, but ultimately is kept healthy. The wolves get fed. Both herd and wolves bed down happy.

Life seems to compete with death, but death is life's strategy for continual rejuvenation through reproduction. Now the importance of fungi is obvious, for without their ability to dismantle the corpses and structures that life once used, the world would soon fill up with detritus. Through their dismantling, they create a soft, spongy seedbed of humus for new plants to grow in. Although fungi seem to compete with living things, trying to rot and destroy them, they are cooperating on a higher, or deeper, level with the whole scheme of life itself.

Not only do the fungi cooperate, they also offer their mushrooms as food to the living. But because they represent the side of death, some mushrooms are deadly poisonous. If a person makes a mistake and eats a deadly mushroom, then falls dead upon the ground, fellow fungi will soon set to work on the body.

Are mushrooms the fungi's trap for unwary or unwitting animals? Could fungi be tempting us with morels, then further offering the deadly amanita for our delectation and death?

Strawberries

*T*he year we were married, Marilyn and I put a hundred-plant strawberry bed behind the old farmhouse we were renting. We kept it weedfree all summer and positioned the plants' runners so that new plants that appeared at their tips would find unoccupied ground.

That winter, the owners told us we had to be out of the house in a month. So we moved here to Berks County, but not without a pang at leaving our manicured strawberry bed, from which we'd never tasted a berry.

Anyone who has planted up a decent-sized strawberry bed knows that it's a chore one won't willingly repeat. It took us many years before we were ready to plant strawberries again. Then, five years ago, a friend gave us a package of a hundred strawberry plants. A vacant spot in the garden was just the right size for the patch, so we spent the day putting them in.

Every plant grew. And that first year, every plant threw out many runners, filling the patch solid with strawberry leaves. The next spring we had a bumper crop, and each of the strawberry plants celebrated by throwing out many more runners. I saw the bed getting crowded, but I never found the time to get in there and clean it out. The third year, the berry harvest was down, as strawberry plants occupied every square inch of ground. The fourth year, last year, berries were hard to find and the bed was clogged with many, many small plants. This spring, the strawberries are gone, having multiplied themselves into choking mats of roots and runners that finally collapsed under their own fecundity.

The commands going out to the runners from the mother plant say: "Find a piece of bare soil and grow!" There's no feedback from the runners saying, "There's no more room out here. Rootability zero!" Feedback from the runners would give the mother plant a way to regulate runner production, to fill the available space around her and then stop.

Strawberries are plants that colonize disturbed soil. They soak up the sun until shrubs and trees grow back and close their leaf canopy, returning the forest floor to permanent shade. As such, strawberries' imperative is to cover as much ground as possible. They need no feedback system from the runners. This is ambition unchecked and it's only good for a few years until it burns itself out.

There also comes a time in human life when ambition can cause serious harm, when the imperative to succeed can lead people to cut corners, shave points, and manipulate friendships. But unlike the strawberry plant, we get feedback from our actions. We know when we've hurt someone, even though we may rationalize it as a necessary side effect of getting what we want.

If we become caught up with achieving success at all costs, we lose our perspective. We no longer see ourselves in the larger human context, just as the ever-multiplying strawberries don't recognize the approaching conditions of their own demise.

Yet we humans have an extraordinary—if often neglected—faculty for seeing ourselves with detachment, objectively, in a context larger than personal desires or concerns. This faculty operates in the deepest place within us—where we can be silent, passionless, and aware of everything. When viewing life through those cool eyes, we neither fall into despondency nor become wildly elated. We are not then engaged in life, but rather viewing our actions from the heights of our value system—the higher the values, the farther we can see, and the more perspective we get on our actions.

When the strawberries got too thick, I should have tilled every other row into the ground and destroyed them, allowing fresh ground for new runners to root in. The following year, I should have tilled the rows I'd left the previous year. In this way, no row of strawberries would be more than two years old.

Similarly, when we get too close to the world and find ourselves getting tangled and choked by our rampant desires, we need to find our dispassionate eyes. Then we'll see our wants in the larger picture, and if they are inconsequential or merely selfish, we can root them out mercilessly.

Tulip Poplar

*T*he dominant tree in our woods is the tulip poplar, *Liriodendron tulipifera.* It's also called yellow poplar, tulip tree, and telephone pole tree.

The lore in these parts is that the telephone company uses tulip poplar for poles because it grows so straight and tall, but I'm skeptical.

I didn't always feel this way. When we moved here, I was greatly impressed by a huge specimen, over 3 feet in diameter and 80 feet tall, no more than 25 feet from the garage. It looked so ponderous and mighty. With its crown high above the surrounding trees, it surveyed the whole property. That tree, I thought, must be the oldest living thing on the place, the founder of the present ecosystem, never to be cut or damaged.

That first summer here, we chain-sawed down three tall, straight poplars growing right in the middle of what was to be our garden. I noticed then that the saw worked unusually easily in the soft wood. Later, the stumps sent up dozens of suckers that reached 4 inches in diameter in one year. I cut them off again, wishing the stumps would die. Poplars, I saw, grow like weeds.

A further impression of the wood came the following winter, when I used it in the woodstove. I'd sawed the felled trees into logs and stacked them. Despite the girth of the logs, they were surprisingly light, and I wondered if they'd give much heat. Yet the flood tide of poplar on the porch gave me assurance of enough wood for the whole heating season.

The dried poplar was even lighter, like sturdy balsa wood. It was easy to split and I had plenty, and soon the logs were snapping and popping in the fireplace. Now I knew why it was called poplar. It rends the air and the ear with tiny explosions, and if the woodstove door is open, throws smoldering red sparks onto the rugs and floor.

Poplar burns in a trice. Its anemic BTU count barely warmed our living room. I remembered a time I'd used apple wood in a stove, how wonderful the apple smelled, and how bright, hot, and long-lasting its fire had been. Poplar, I discovered, smelled like the Sunday papers burning. And the only way to get the woodstove cranking on the coldest nights was to stoke it every half hour. I'd burned the porchful of poplar by mid-January.

These experiences gave me a new sense of the giant tree by the garage. Now I saw it as overblown papier-mâché, most likely rotten at the core. If other big poplars I'd seen cut down were typical, then the bigger they come, the more likely they are to have their centers turn to brown peat. I saw their strategy: Go for size and skimp on wood; reach the canopy and dominate; forget a strong structure.

Tulip poplars play the hare to the oak trees' tortoise, for oaks will eventually shoulder out these flimsy giants, and do it with wood that's twice as dense. It's rare, though, to find woods where the oaks have muscled out the poplars because the farmers around here know what mature oaks will bring at the sawmill. If an oak grows to a dominant size, it's cut down. Poplar, on the other hand, is often ignored, and so it dominates. The big poplar that flanks the garage is impressive in size, but not nearly as impressive as a similarly sized oak would be.

The living part of any tree is the cambium, a thin film of tissue a few cells thick that sheathes the wood. On its outside surface, it produces bark. On its inside, it makes wood. The wood is the tree's history—the bones of seasons past. But the cambium is its flesh, and if scraped from the wood of my giant poplar, it probably wouldn't fill a gallon jug.

It's no different with people. The past into which memory goes is wood—solidified, unchangeable, structural. The only living part of us is here in the present, an evanescent presence that just touches each moment, then is gone. And with each touch, the moment is frozen in time, then stored away. We who are lucky enough to be alive fly with the present for the span of our lives, creating the past as we go. Some day this wood will be tested. Some, like the poplar, will prove lightweight and rotten at the core. Some, like the oak, will be sound, and fit for further work.

Morning
Glories

"*T*ime began in a garden" says the metal plaque by the entrance to my friend's garden. The words stopped me.

Time—the human concept of time—began when humans began. The image of Adam and Eve in the garden came to mind. The first humans found themselves in the flow of time that coursed through Eden. Whether one thinks of the first humans as a literal Adam and Eve, or as hominids that first gained access to reflective mind, they found themselves in nature's garden. Their reflective minds knew that they knew. Their present moments were colored by knowledge of the past and speculation about the future.

The past is very real to people, even though we know that reality resides only in the eternal present, which is eternally changing. Because of the reflective mind, people see patterns of change as they live through the succession of present moments. From these patterns emerge our perceptions of time.

The regular changes of the circling sun, moon, and stars must have been among the first patterns recognized by the first humans. Or perhaps they noticed the morning glories.

As a child, I didn't understand that morning glories only open in the morning and close by the time lunch is finished. I loved their happy blue color and satiny trumpets, which I'd tear to little bits and toss in the air, like pieces of the sky. Sometime during my journey to adulthood, I realized the meaning of their name. Early man must have also slowly associated the time function of morning glories with their absence in the afternoon.

But did early man have morning glories? Our common variety Heavenly Blue is a cultivated type of *Ipomoea purpurea*, the wild morning glory that troubles crops like corn, beans, and cotton. Its wild relative, field bindweed (*Convolvulus arvensis*), is even more of a pest, and has also been bred for flowers. Both have white, wormlike roots that break easily, each piece having the regenerative power to grow a new plant. Tilling and plowing only spread them. The wild morning glories are survivors, and with over 1,500 species found throughout the world in both temperate and tropical zones, it's likely that early man did indeed see morning glories, noticed them opening and closing on schedule, and grasped their past, present, and future. Thus time began.

Marilyn and I always plant Heavenly Blue. Few other flowers are so lush and exuberant as this variety's big blue blossoms. The blue suddenly changes to flowing gold in the flower's throat, making the whole blossom resemble a yellow sun in a blue sky.

We dress the utility pole by our toolshed with these twisty vines. Years ago we wound a tough piece of steel strapping around the pole to give the morning glories a firm grasp for climbing. As they wind upward, flowers appear as small buds that look like unicorn horns. Just after dawn, when the day brightens, they unfurl their delicate trumpets to greet the sun.

Flowers last just one morning, then shrivel away, to be followed by seed. In some places the plant will self-sow, but it never does for us. We treat it like an annual, and if we get it out early enough in the season, it will bloom from summer until the frosts claim it in October.

By the afternoon the vines look bedraggled from their morning's effort and the leaves wilt easily in the hot summer sun. But I know that tomorrow morning they will be as colorful and fresh as they were this morning.

Time begins anew for us each day, when we wake from the strange land of sleep that lies outside of time and space. I rub my eyes open and head down the ladder from the sleeping loft to begin the day. I can see the pole by the toolshed through the window as I descend. The pole is covered with a cloud of Heavenly Blue. My foggy morning mind is concerned with the simple things. Hungers and urges impel me forward. I am early man. After my morning coffee, I will become civilized man. But now I stand by the window, half in dreamland, responding to my family with a grunt.

I see the morning glories, and I can feel time begin.

Dame's
Rocket

*D*riving home from work one day in May shortly after we moved to our current property, I spied bunches of pretty white and violet flowers growing along the roadside. I picked a bouquet for Marilyn. Now, twelve years later, the plant is everywhere at our place. Perhaps the plant became established when seeds from that first bouquet fell to the ground and sprouted. It wasn't here when we moved in.

The plant began blooming the next year in one small patch behind the doghouse. When we tore down the doghouse and developed that spot into our crystal garden, we must have spread the plant by tossing its roots and seedpods into the woods as we weeded the freshly dug soil.

At first we called the plant phlox, because it looks like phlox. But we found that while the florets of phlox have five petals, this plant has only four. And there are subtle differences in the leaves as well. Besides, the plant grows 3 feet tall, and the 3-foot-tall phlox, *Phlox paniculata*, doesn't bloom until later in the summer. We finally identified it as dame's rocket (*Hesperis matronalis*).

Hesperis smells like violets—a sweet but faint odor. The flowers range from white to purple on different stems, with many shades of light violet, violet, and pinkish violet in between. A patch that naturalized around the stump of the old catalpa tree has made a genetic leap: Its green leaves are mottled with yellow and its flowers are variegated with markings of white and reddish purple in small, intricate designs.

The botanical name, *Hesperis matronalis*, could be translated as dame's hesperis. Hesperis was one of the Hesperides, the mythic Greek "daughters of the evening." She and her two sisters, Aegle and Erytheia, guarded a tree bearing golden apples far away in the twilit West. I think of that as I stand by the garden in the evening, when the sun has set and the long May twilight is lingering. Because dame's rocket likes moist spots in light shade, the plant's white and light violet colors glow against the pools of darkness gathered in the woods. Violet and purple are brighter to our eyes in twilight than in full daylight, and so the hesperis glows even brighter as the evening passes. Finally, at nightfall, it's the last flower seen. "Daughter of the Evening" is inspired nomenclature, for it's then that the plant shows most brilliantly and beautifully.

We favor blue flowers in our late May garden— *Iris sibirica*, for instance, and perennial blue flax, hardy geraniums, and aquilegias, right on down to ground covers like *Mazus reptans*, which hoists tiny, flaring flowers of the same hue as hesperis.

Dame's rocket has come unbidden to add a natural grace note to our plantings. It surrounds the crystal garden where Marilyn placed glistening slabs of quartz crystal-encrusted rock that she found in

Arkansas. The hesperis has sprung up to completely cover the wreckage of the spring bulb garden's ratty-looking leaves. Up by the vegetable garden, it has covered the compost pile and environs, and down by the springhouse it borders the deep shade of the woods beyond.

Marilyn and I thought we had finished our gardens last year, but in retrospect something was lacking. This year, I see what it was. As we were working toward completion, so was Nature, in the form of her hesperis. This year Nature considered what we had wrought and exploded everywhere with her own finishing touch, the sweet afterthought of dame's rocket.

False Solomon's Seal

Our most spectacular garden of perennials used to be a rough, weedy bank held together with the tough roots of greenbrier, multiflora rose, choke-cherries, and poison ivy. Other denizens of waste places grew there, too, such as mayapple, black-berry, and false Solomon's seal (*Smilacina racemosa*).

Although the latter group of wildings seems to be the weaker, mayapples to this day open their umbrellas among the yarrows we planted. Black-berry roots persist down under the edge of a huge rock we uncovered, and send up their succulent, thorny shoots every year. False Solomon's seal never died out in a spot just below two other large rocks we revealed when we dug out the bank. The worst of the wild weeds have long been chased out of the garden, and good riddance. I'd like to see that lone blackberry go, too. But I've grown fond of the few mayapple parasols that linger. And this year I dis-covered great virtue in the false Solomon's seal.

Smilacina is distinguished from true Solomon's seal by its zigzag stem and by its flowers. Solomon's seal (*Polygonatum biflorum*) blooms along the length of its stem, while smilacina produces feath-ery plumes at the tips of its stems, followed later by red berries. Our specimen is now blushing golden yellow at the tips of its white clusters of starry florets. A close look shows the florets on the clusters to be gold until they open creamy white. Since the florets at the tips open last, the clusters look like they're dipped in butter at this stage of their flowering.

In years past, because it was a wild plant for which I had no garden plan, I'd pull off the tops of the smilacina as I weeded the area below the big rocks. Last year we divided a large stand of *Iris siberica*, deep blue irises that open about 2 feet above the ground, and extended the drift to the area where the false Solomon's seal grows.

This year the irises are up and blooming well, joined by a single early yellow daylily and the old smilacina that refused to leave. The yellow and white smilacina plumes and the lemon yellow daylily relieve and enhance the large, dark mass of blue iris. Here's a perfect combination of plants— not only do the colors harmonize, but the smilacina's broad, creased, and wavy-edged leaves contrast well with the thin, straight blades of the iris and daylily.

What gives me pause is the knowledge that the plant I tried to eradicate has assumed a starring role in our otherwise routine design, lifting it to high horticultural art. If a visitor with a strong aesthetic sense tours our gardens and sees the way smilacina consorts with iris and daylily, he or she will certainly assume we planned the arrangement and give us high, if undeserved, marks. Thus providence enhances human endeavors.

I see the same enhancement happening when we cultivate the inner person and make a garden of ourselves.

Wild tendencies that spring from the primal part of us, from the ancient animals that coil within us, are like the tough-rooted wild plants that confronted us when we moved here.

Some, such as jealousy and hate, should be dug out by the roots and eradicated forever. Others, like the sexual urge, need to be kept trimmed back lest they take over the garden, but certainly not eradicated. Sexual hunger, if kept in its proper place, will add a wild and free beauty to our cultivated virtues, as smilacina has done for our irises and daylily.

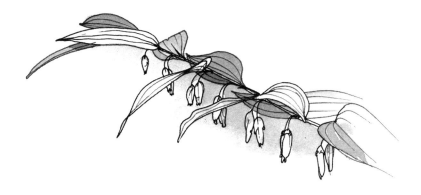

Blueberries

*B*lueberries are native to the Pocono Plateau in eastern Pennsylvania, where I grew up. They favor burnt-over patches of the scrubby oak forest that covers a county-sized slough atop the high plateau. Nature has chosen blueberries for a featured role in the succession of plants that returns the land to climax forest in this windy, elevated, boggy place.

Under the protection of the blueberry bushes, trees get their start. Within a few years the trees grow above and shade the bushes, cutting down on berry production. Folks native to the area often supplemented their income by picking the wild berries for sale to fruit wholesalers, and early on discovered that forest fires would clear the trees nicely, and that the land would grow back to blueberries. Fires, most of them set, were thus common over the high plateau in summer.

Sometimes the blueberry fires got out of hand. In the early 1950s, Blue Mountain, a few miles south of our home, caught fire. The mountain is a 2,000-foot ridge running northeast to southwest, and the top of that ridge was the rim of my young world. During the first day of the fire, I could see a flat cloud of smoke pouring up from the top of the mountain. That night, as darkness deepened, the scene grew menacing. Now I could see a broad red glow, underlighting the billowing smoke, punctuated with little white flashes that I knew must be whole trees bursting into flame. My neighbors were practicing slash and burn agriculture, without the slash.

Before the 1920s, blueberries came only from the wild. Southern New Jersey was prime blueberry country. The acid, boggy soil of the Pine Barrens suited their needs. The Pocono soil was similarly acid, favoring rhododendron and mountain laurel along with blueberries. These berries were somewhat smaller and a little tastier than the New Jersey kind. From these and other strains, breeders developed our modern commercial varieties.

The blueberry's cousin, the huckleberry, shares its range in the Poconos. Huckleberries are about a half to a third the size of blueberries, but seem to carry the same amount of flavor. A few years ago, Marilyn and I drove to Blue Mountain to hike part of the Appalachian Trail and discovered a large patch of huckleberries in a burnt-over spot. We brought home enough to make a huckleberry pie that to this day remains the benchmark against which all subsequent pies are measured.

Our current home is 50 miles south of the high plateau, and 35 miles south of Blue Mountain, and in quite a different ecosystem. Even so, the five commercial blueberry bushes we've planted are healthy and wealthy with fruit. To make them feel even more at home, we plaster the ground around them with mats of newspapers in the spring, then shovel wood chips over the paper. The newspapers soak up a lot of moisture and keep the soil damp. As they and the chips decay, the soil becomes more acid.

My blueberries are host to one of the cleverest pieces of plant life around, the mummy-berry fungus. It causes me no great problems, but affects one bush that is mostly in the shade. According to USDA researchers, this fungus can reproduce only if it gets off the leaves and onto the flowers of the blueberry.

To accomplish this, it has come up with a remarkable scheme for turning a leaf into a mock flower that attracts pollinators. Its spores then ride on the pollinator's feet as it moves on to the real flowers. The fungus first invades the leaf and wilts it to disguise its shape, then forces the leaf to exude sugars and emit a fragrant aroma. When the researchers looked at these wilted leaves under ultraviolet light (the range in which many pollinators see), the fungi's mock flower was marked the way real flowers are, to facilitate identification and insect landings. Do pollinators fall for this cockamamie scheme? All the time, as the mummies among my ripe berries attest.

Compared to the wild blueberries of the high plateau, my garden varieties look a little out of place, gussied up and fancified as they are for commercial distribution. Yet they're not many generations from the wild—like the men with plaid shirts and rifles who used to set the woods afire.

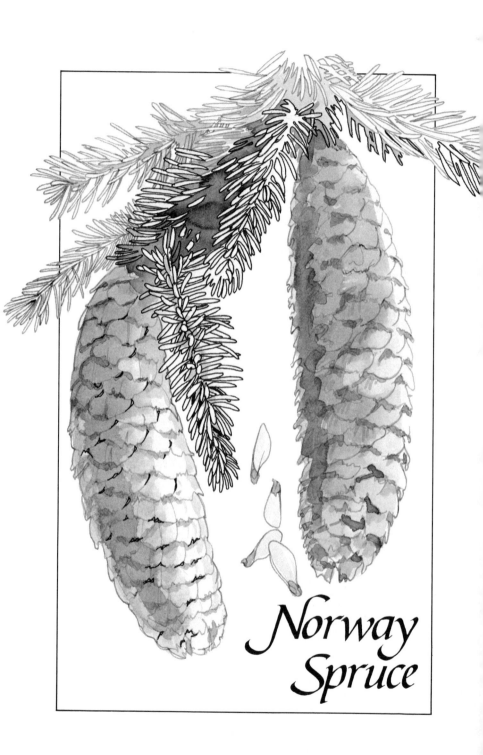

Norway Spruce

*W*hen we moved here, one of our first jobs was to free the area around the house from the overgrowth of old trees that generations of our predecessors had planted.

From the house to the toolshed—no more than 60 feet—were four large black walnuts, severely crowding each other. We cut down the middle two trees. Across from the front porch a huge, half-rotten catalpa hung its giant, beanlike swords above our heads. I cut it down. Also culled were a scruffy white pine, two tulip poplars, and several young hickories.

We decided to leave two mature, gorgeous specimens of Norway spruce that were revealed when the catalpa came down, even though they threw a tremendous amount of shade. Thank goodness we saved them, for these trees have become very important to us.

Nine years ago we built an 8-by-8-foot skylight in our roof, under which is our sleeping loft. We wake to see the Norway spruces against the sky. In the winter, they fill the picture with green, and when it snows, they become soft sculpture. In the fall, squirrels come to gather the long, papery cones with two seeds behind each scale. We spend a few extra minutes in bed when these furry little aerialists show up.

In the spring the trees burst out with fancy light green buds of new needles at the tip of each twig. In the hot summer their huge pool of shade contributes to the coolness around our old stone house. At every time of the year their shaggy presence is at once paternal and primordial.

The other day, in bed, dreamily staring out of the skylight, I turned my head and thought I saw, out of the corner of my eye, a squirrel run along a branch high in the larger of the two spruces. I turned my head again, and again something ran squirrel-like along the limb. It was no squirrel, but rather an imperfection in the plastic skylight.

I wondered how an aborigine might interpret this scene. To him, it would appear that something was moving in the tree—he would not understand about the clear plastic between himself and the tree. He would believe that the imperfection was in the tree and not in his own perception.

How often we judge other people's imperfections, sure that the fault is in them. Perhaps it's not. It may be that our criticisms stem from an imperfection in us, in the way we see the world.

When I stand outside and look at the trees through clear air, they are perfect.

Campanula

*W*hy, after all, is June the month for weddings? Is it because spring's youthful, verdant rush is maturing into the season of flowers and fruit, symbolizing the fecundity of young men and women? Perhaps, but I prefer to think that wedding bells ring in June because that's when the bellflowers appear—perfect floral symbols of marriage.

The prettiest campanula we grow is *Campanula persicifolia* 'Alba,' Canterbury bells. Its 1-inch, pure white bells seem like the decorations on a wedding cake come to life. Just a few feet away in the sunny garden is *Campanula glomerata*, the deep violet, spiky-looking clustered bellflower. Fifty feet from these, in a shady garden, grows *Campanula rotundifolia* 'Olympica,' called bluebells of Scotland. From a densely matted center the size of a saucer, this campanula sends out dozens of trailing, wiry stems with thin foliage. It hangs the most evocative blue bells from these stems. The blue is softly electric and glows faintly in the deep shade. The stems find their proper light levels by settling in among the foliage of nearby plants. Whatever flowers may be blooming above, bluebells of Scotland hang like ornaments from the foliage below.

On a ledge above Olympica grows *Campanula carpatica* 'Blue Chips,' called Carpathian harebell. This plant makes small mounds of toothed, heart-shaped leaves and hangs out many light blue bells from June through September. Last November, in fact, both Olympica and Blue Chips were still ringing a few last bells before the night of the long winter descended on them.

Because most campanulas have a mass of fibrous roots, they are fairly easily dug up in the spring, pulled apart into divisions, and replanted. They're also an easy plant to give away, as people tend to fall in love with the dainty blue bells of the shade-loving varieties and the bold statements made by the sun-loving types.

Here in eastern Pennsylvania, where the Pennsylvania Dutch are the cultural progenitors, custom has it that you're not supposed to say thanks for the gift of a plant, or, I've heard it said, the plant won't grow. These Pennsylvania Germans ("Dutch" is a misnomer) are generally a courteous people, so it seems strange that such a custom would arise.

Perhaps the taboo arose because we use courtesy to oil the interface between ourselves and acquaintances in daily life, courtesy that's not necessary when a gift is given from the heart, as most gifts of plants are given. Or maybe it arose because saying thanks would in some way offend the plant, or the deva of the plant. Let's be silent about the plant, lest it steal away.

The gift of a plant is a token of love. A little treasure of life is shared with a friend or lover. You need nothing in return, because though you give your plant away, you still have your plant. We can divide campanulas for visiting friends *ad infinitum* and still have plenty. Love is like that. It's possible to love more than one person with your whole heart, as my relationship with my four children has taught me, and still have a heart-full left over.

The very names of many flowers resound with the theme of love. Infatuation begins with Cupid's dart (*Catananche caerulea*), turning ordinary young people into helpless innocents, unable to resist passion. Passion's embrace is represented by love-in-a-mist, the beautiful, bushy plant with moody blue flowers set amid fine leaves.

As often happens in love, the couple parts, and forget-me-nots (*Myosotis sylvestris*) are passed from hand to hand. As also happens, somebody usually forgets. Now bleeding heart (*Dicentra spectabilis*) is the appropriate symbol, or, if the case of heartbreak is a particularly bad one, love-lies-bleeding (*Amaranthus caudatus*).

If all this heavy Victorian swooning seems too much, the lighthearted among us can go for love-in-a-puff (*Cardiospermum halicacabum*) and let it go at that.

Gas
Plant

*M*r. Searfoss was just solving the equation when the room shook, glass crashed to the floor, and a tremendous boom left an eerie silence in its wake. The ninth graders began to express astonishment, but Mr. Searfoss stood frozen at the board with the pointer in his hand.

My hand shot up. He nodded at me. "Can I go to the boy's room?" I asked. My request didn't fool him. "Yes, you can go see what happened," he laughed.

I ducked out of the school building and ran toward a column of smoke hanging over the next block. As I got closer, people were running and milling about. Around the corner, the street glittered with glass, then disappeared under a jagged jumble of shattered wood. Capping this woodpile was the entire roof of the house that had blown up a few minutes before. All this hove up before me in the street, like a shipwreck. The lot where the house had been was a smoking hole in the ground. I went back to class and reported all this; much to everyone's interest, I had gotten away with leaving school property during school hours. It was my first taste of journalism's special freedoms.

It turned out that a leak had filled the house with cooking gas and a spark had set the thing off like a bomb. Nobody was home, and nobody was injured. The incident gave me a big respect for gas stoves when I encountered them in various houses and apartments in later years.

Once a man came to fix our gas stove. He had no eyebrows. Said it was an occupational hazard.

And so it was with some interest that I came across a cartoon of *Dictamnus albus* 'Rubra' in a seed catalog several years ago. "Amazing Gas Plant" said the caption, with that slight hysteria peculiar to advertisements for horticultural novelties. The drawing showed a flower stalk with many blossoms, a gas flame burning from the tip of each one.

I dismissed this as nonsense and forgot about the gas plant until one day last year, when a particularly beautiful flower spike arose between clumps of bachelor's buttons. It was a gas plant that Marilyn had put in, unbeknownst to me, three years before. The plant is slow to mature and sinks a taproot that resents being moved. I tried to light one of its blossoms, holding my lighter just in front of the opened flower. Nothing happened.

This past June I was again surprised by the beauty of our dictamnus. This year it was twice as large as last and three times more floriferous. At dusk I found myself in the garden, admiring its rose-pink flowers, when I got a whiff of a fresh, citrusy smell, like a squeezed grapefruit or lemon rind. Above the opened flowers at the bottom of the spike were half-opened buds, chambers with small holes at the tip. The evening was very still, with no wind. Why not try it again?

Out came the lighter. As the fire approached a half-opened bud, a jet of flame spit from the end of the bud with a little *phfft* of combustion. I tried several more, and they *phfft*-ed also. Then I held the flame before the fully opened buds. No *phfft*. From the citrusy smell, I deduced that the plant produced a volatile oil which was concentrated in the chambers of the buds, and the vapors of which were combustible.

Although I was delighted to find the legend true, the effect was certainly nothing like the advertisement showing flowers burning away like gaslights.

We deal with an enormous amount of such hype in modern life. We soon learn that reality is far less grandiose, yet much more interesting, than it's painted by merchandisers. Most of us know, or have met, a few celebrities in our lives. I've found most of them to be very ordinary people, albeit with some extraordinary aspect or talent that has brought the eye of the media upon them. The truly extraordinary human beings I've encountered are usually people whose impact is local, yet profound.

The gas plant is really much more interesting for its beautiful flowers than for its ability to manufacture combustible gas. Its "shtick" is advertised, while its true beauty goes unrecognized until the gardener suddenly discovers the local, profound impact of the blooms.

Nodding
Thistle

$\mathcal{F}$ar from cultivating the thistle, I joined a running battle against all the local representatives of the clan the day I moved here, and I've been running and battling ever since.

Although Canada thistle, *Cirsium arvense*, has been under attack here for over ten years, I could walk you to the garden right now and find one trying to sneak back into the pampered soil to spew its paratrooping seeds everywhere.

When I see these infiltrators I try to pull out the whole root, which always proves impossible, since the roots are long, tender, and wind through the soil. I content myself with pulling out as much as I can, but I pay for it later: Pinched-off Canada thistles grow two or three smaller crowns from each root.

In thirty-seven states it's a crime to let Canada thistle grow on your property, so the gardener's rules must be: Don't go on vacation when the thistles are flowering. Watch for their purplish pink flowers. Cut out the whole plant.

After years of filling my fingers with microfine thistle needles, I've learned how to handle them without getting stung. As you grasp the stem, keep your hand moving toward the growing tip while applying pressure and the needles will lie down under your fingers. If you grasp them straight on, or with movement toward the base of the plant, you'll be sorry. Thistle stems are rather weak and often only the top comes off. When that happens I use a second technique for pulling thistles without getting hurt: I pull back the soil from the very base of the plant and grasp the part of the stem that had been under the soil. Thistles put out protective spines only on aerial parts.

From time to time, in early spring, I come across the basal rosettes of *Carduus nutans*, the nodding thistle. Leaves of this species are deeply lobed, and each lobe is tipped with a fine white thorn. They remind me of crabs in the grass, ready to bite, and I gouge them out by kicking backwards with the sharp edge of my bootheel.

This past spring I saw one of these basal rosettes growing along the woodsy edge of a shady path to the upper gardens. Marilyn's crystal garden borders the other side of the path. I thought about kicking the thistle out, but it was strangely handsome: The tips of the leaf lobes were silvery, giving the plant a strongly variegated look, like the flashing of knives in the woods. It made such a striking picture that I allowed it to grow.

Now it's late June, and guess who's the star of all the plants on our property? Nodding thistle gets the nod. At 6½ feet tall, with foot-long silver swords at the base and 3-inch rose-purple flower balls swinging from the tops of tall stems, it is without doubt the most dramatic plant here. Each purple puff has a circling yellow and black bee telling time on its face, and will later have the yellow and black goldfinch plucking its seeds. Although it came unbidden, the thistle anchors the back of the crystal garden and perfectly completes the composition formed by the garden's permanent plants.

The decision to let this specimen grow was an aesthetic one. It paid off. But now the promethean danger nears, for I can't let it set seed or thistles will take me over. I love the flowers, but I must cut them down in full bloom—before the first paratroopers bail out.

Nodding thistle reminds me of the kind of person who, from time to time, turns up unbidden in our lives, shows us a dramatic, exciting personality, then flashes his thorns at us if we get familiar. It's the cowboy, the loner, the rebel without a cause who's most like the thistle. Most often wisdom dictates that we leave such people alone, but it may be we can cultivate a respectful friendship and enjoy the display, as long as we don't get too close.

Ginkgo

Two hundred and fifty million years ago, the order Ginkgoales comprised many kinds of gymnosperms and covered vast areas of the earth. Since then, the dinosaurs have come and gone, flowering plants have appeared, the order Mammalia has spawned a true marvel, humankind, and every species of ginkgo but one has disappeared from the earth.

That remaining species, *Ginkgo biloba*, is no longer found growing wild. It missed extinction only because it was kept alive as a rarity in the arboreta of Chinese and Japanese rulers. When the Orient opened trade with the West, the ginkgo headed to the cities and parks of Europe and America, where it still is a widely seen ornamental tree, known for its toughness, resistance to insects and diseases, and its anachronistic ability to withstand airborne pollution.

Several years ago, Marilyn brought home a flimsy black plastic pot with a stick protruding from the soil and mentioned that it was a ginkgo. We put it up by the composting area while I pondered where it might go. Ginkgoes grow to 130 feet, with trunks 8 feet in diameter, when they like the climate, although in eastern Pennsylvania they probably don't reach half that size. Still, that's a full-sized tree, and we don't have room for many of those. My pondering went for nought, and the ginkgo stayed in the pot for the summer, getting only rainwater to drink. It stayed there for the winter and struggled through the next summer, neglected in its plastic pot, and dried to near-extinction. Then it froze and thawed through another winter above ground. Last spring, I was cleaning up the area by the compost pile when I found the pot back among the weeds. The gingko was still just a whip, but it appeared to be alive, so I decided to take pity on it and plant it.

I pulled the roots from the cracking pot, dug out some handfuls of rich earth where an old compost pile had been, and finally, with a feeling of sympathetic relief, tucked its starving roots into the ground. Then I filled the planting hole depression with 2 gallons of water and forgot about it.

This morning I wandered up by the compost area and noticed that the ginkgo was looking very cheerful. On close inspection, it was beyond cheerful—it was ecstatic. Near the top of its slim stem it had put out some exuberant leaves, 2½ inches across. If a plant can look happy, this one did. I felt a rush of gratitude from the plant, and a happiness to be alive and thriving. In a little vision, it showed me its destiny, and I peered into the future to see it large and vigorous, with the weeds kept down and flowers planted around its base. There was a different family living here, people I didn't know—or didn't yet know. For them, the old ginkgo was a featured tree and rightly so. With its fan-shaped leaves that turn golden yellow in autumn, and its long history, it deserved the attention it was getting. I realized that the family had no idea how or when the ginkgo arrived, but it pleased me to know that I had a hand in their pleasure, though I was long gone.

Time ran backwards and I again cherished the little tree before me. I could see how *Ginkgo biloba* kept going when every other ginkgo in the world died out. It has heart and will, in its vegetative way. It carries a piece of the Permian past forward in time to me, and links me to the future. This tree is powerful. Planting it may have been the smartest thing I've yet done on this land.

Apples

When I have a fixed idea it takes a heap of persuading to get me to change my mind. One needs to muster a lot of energy to thaw the frozen lake of my ideas so that they may flow into new forms. For many years, for instance, I did not see nature's magic.

I began to see the magic in nature when I moved here and started working hands-on with the land and its creatures. For example, when pruning one of my Smokehouse apples, I soon got beyond the basic rules of pruning (remove crossed limbs, keep the middle open, cut limbs close to the wood they arise from) and began shaping and thinning out the tree as if I were giving it an artistic haircut. Something didn't feel right about that, so in subsequent years, I learned to look at each limb and branch from the tree's point of view.

Of what use was the branch? Was it a future fruit-bearer or was it diverting energy needed farther out the limb? It felt right to think for the tree. It could very well be that we humans are graced with intelligence in order to think for, and apply our minds to, the flora and fauna—for their betterment, not ours.

After a few years of actively thinking for my tree when pruning it, there came to me one day a soft suggestion to stop thinking altogether. I was standing amid the Smokehouse's lower limbs, loppers in hand, when I decided to follow the suggestion. My hands fell to my sides and I relaxed. The whole day

came to life: The cawing of distant crows, the chitter
of red squirrels, and the sound of the wind formed a
cavernous aural landscape. The March sun warmed
my arms. The busy quiet of the countryside surrounded me.

Now I had a hunch that the tree would be better
without a particular branch, so I lopped it off. I went
over the whole tree that way, cutting when it felt
right, feeling right about my hunches. I've used this
method ever since, and have reached the point
where I simply let the tree tell me where it wants
pruning.

My definition of magic is when hunches pan out.
One of the apple varieties in my orchard was discovered with the help of nature's magic. In 1838, Mrs.
Richard Cox, wife of an English country clergyman,
walked from her back door into her yard. Her large
apple tree was in full bloom, and she stopped to
drink in the light floral fragrance of the blossoms,
the color, and the sound of the bees. She was enrap-
tured by this scene, especially by one bee working a
flower right in front of her. As she watched the bee
gathering nectar, she later said that the scene became a symbol for the whole plan of life. She somehow knew that that flower was very special. Using a
piece of thread, she marked the blossom. Over the
summer, the blossom developed into an apple, and
when she picked it, she saved its five seeds. It took
many years to grow all five seeds to trees of fruiting
size, but she followed it through. Four of the apples
from these five trees were of good but ordinary quality. The fruit from the fifth tree was a miracle—the
best-tasting apple she or her husband—or their
neighbors—had ever eaten. Within a few years, it
was judged the best-tasting apple in all of England,

and the Cox Orange Pippin is still considered by many to be the finest and most aromatic of all apples, with a fresh, clean taste. Mrs. Cox's original wood has been vegetatively propagated over the years and I'm happy to have a piece of it on my land.

Where do these hunches come from? I believe that they originate, in part, in the plants themselves. Something about the plant suggests to an open mind new possibilities for form and function, and our mind takes it from there. A hunch is a feeling, and the feeling is magic. A connection is being made between the gardener and the plant on a level beyond our everyday consciousness. And it doesn't just happen with apple trees. For the gardener who believes in magic, it happens all the time.

There are those who feel that all human knowledge of plants has been hard won by the trials and errors of farmers and scientists over the centuries, and that we are the beneficiaries of their work. We prune according to principles human minds have discovered from watching the dumb, programmed responses of the trees to pruning. There is no magic about it. It would be foolish to be caught by the sight of a bee and an apple blossom. It would be silly to mark the blossom with a thread, and save the seeds of the apple it produced.

But in applying what we learn, we eventually reach a point where we reinvent what we're doing. We see beyond the rules to the reason for the rules. Once we see that, we become flexible, impressionable, open. It's then that we see the magic in the ordinary, as Mrs. Cox saw magic in a busy bee. The magic is always working; we just are seldom ready to perceive it.

Rose Campion

*T*he lurid rose-magenta flowers and silver-grey leaves of rose campion (*Lychnis coronaria*) make a picture by themselves and tend to overwhelm other flowers nearby. So gardeners usually find a spot off by itself for the plant.

Marilyn, however, placed our rose campion among blue-flowered bachelor's buttons this year, and not long ago I discovered her startling combination and saw its colors blaze in the full sun. Using the artist's trick of squinting at the picture to reduce it to masses of flat colors, I was surprised to see the campion's red and the bachelor's buttons' blue stand out from the murky background and shimmer with light. Although of different hues, their vibrancy and intensity were equal.

A line of *Veronica spicata*'s white spikes held these glowing dots of color in check, sealing them off from the more subtle colors nearby. The spikes pointed at the sky, which I noticed was clouding over.

The wind picked up and blew away the muggy, motionless air. The temperature dropped a few degrees. Near the zenith of the sky, big grey clouds crowded their way over the sun, while in the west the sky was already dark and impenetrable. A bird zoomed past me on a long, low arc, then dove into the forest. The breeze felt good, although I knew that in local thunderstorms the wind can get out of hand. Thunder rolled over the hills from far away, and soon a flicker of lightning—surprisingly close—showed in the western sky. The wind grew stronger and I went in the house.

The dog cowered under the table and I listened to the radio, hoping that a bolt wouldn't shatter the power company's circuit breaker on the electrical pole outside, as it had several times before.

Now the thunder and lightning were upon us, and I looked out the window at the dark, storm-tossed world. Trees hurled their arms back and forth. Leaves and bits of detritus flew past. A light flashed, then immediately the thunder crashed in a shuddering report. The lights flickered, went out. The house was strangely quiet and dark, and from the windows, which were suddenly lighter than the inside of the house, I saw big raindrops pattering down. Another flash, then another, and the huge crashes made me grimace. It rained hard now. Thunder started its rolling boom again, denoting distance. The wind died down and a cool, fresh breeze blew through the screens. The lights came back on. The soft rain continued for a few minutes, then subsided, and I went back outside to find the world refreshed, cool, and moist.

A light breeze still blew. Misty leftover rain-drops felt good on my face as I walked back to the upper garden, where I'd left the rose campion. I wanted to see it again, after the rain. In the cloudy aftermath of the storm, it looked sullen, deeper, without that vibrant glow. And the bachelor's buttons looked a bit subdued and bedraggled. The sky was clearing in the west; blue sky was approaching. As the clouds evaporated, the sky above grew lighter, then darker as clouds crossed, then lighter again as they separated. With more light the flowers increased their glow, and with less light, turned dark again.

Large patches of blue sky appeared above, and in a minute the sun peeked out from behind some lingering white clouds, then ducked back again. I saw a flash from the flowers. Twice more the sun played peekaboo with the flowers and then came out for good, in full brilliance.

Suddenly the campion's dull magenta burst into a shimmering deep rose light that leapt from the tops of the flowers. The bachelor's buttons' blue caught fire, a sapphire halo above each flower. The flowers danced with joy to be finished with their bath and their drink, and to be playing in the sun again.

Perhaps it was that my eyes then became over-saturated with color, or the flowers' joy subsided, but they dimmed a bit—to the level I'd encountered before the storm. Now I had to squint again to see them glow. And so, the plants continued their day and I continued mine.

That evening I heard a radio performance of Beethoven's Sixth Symphony, "The Pastorale." The announcer said that Beethoven had not named its five movements at first, feeling that their meaning was obvious to anyone with a familiarity with nature and the countryside. But later he relented and named them thus:

Part I—The countryside, brooks, glens, glades; birds twitter. Part II—The human heart responds to nature's beauty; a cuckoo sings. Part III—A thunderstorm approaches; the storm; lightning flashes; the brooks run tumultuous in their courses. Part IV—The storm subsides and skies clear; the sun appears. Part V—Nature rejoices and gives thanks to the Creator.

As I listened to the last movement, I could hear nature's gratitude swell toward the climactic note of the symphony, a single transcendent note of purity, unity, and joy that lasts less than two seconds, but is set in the symphony's sky like a star by the notes leading up to and away from it. Disney's rendering of this note in *Fantasia* had Apollo driving his fiery chariot across the sky. I realized that my garden had hit that note just that afternoon, when the sun called forth a transcendent dazzle from my rose campion and her associates.

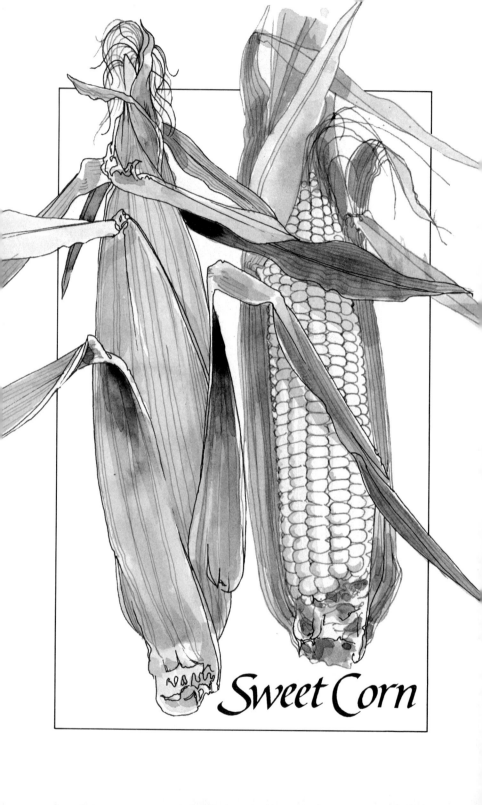

Sweet Corn

J am lucky enough to have had Ben Seem as a neighbor once upon a time. Ben was a Quaker, a seedsman, and a good friend to most people who knew him. He was a tall, lanky fellow with a decisive and opinionated mind, which was turned for most of the time on his 125 acres. There he grew hybrid seed for the big seed companies—corn, wheat, and oats, but mostly corn.

Every August Ben would harvest a special patch of sweet corn he grew well away from his hybrids and deliver a dozen ears to each of his neighbors within a mile of the farm. This gesture was keenly anticipated: The corn was always the freshest, sweetest, most perfect of the season. Although I'm sure Ben enjoyed giving away his corn to be neighborly, he had other reasons, too. He asked us all not to grow any corn in our own gardens, lest the pollen interfere with his hybrids.

Every year when the corn gets ripe, I think of Ben, who died a dozen years ago, and I continue to look for a variety as good as that unknown type he gave away. I'd never found one—until this year.

The white shoepeg types like Stowell's Evergreen, the popular white types like Silver Queen, and many different kinds of yellow varieties all fell

short of Ben's corn. Perhaps the sweetest I'd hereto-
fore tasted was the Illini Xtra Sweet, which has both
yellow and white kernels on its cobs.

Then, just recently, I tasted the 1986 All-
America Selections winner for corn, How Sweet It Is
(White)—a new hybrid. The variety has two to three
times the sugar content of ordinary sweet corn,
along with the useful ability to retain its sweetness
longer than any other known type. How Sweet It Is
takes eighty-five days to mature—not bad for
corn—and carries sixteen to eighteen rows of small,
crispy-sweet, pure white kernels on its cobs.

I'm sure that if Ben Seem were still around, he'd
plant a batch of this corn for his neighbors. Man's
eternal quest for sweeter corn has just advanced
several giant steps.

It used to be that to get corn at peak sweetness,
one would have to get the ears from the stalks to the
boiling pot of water as soon as possible. I remember
one apocryphal story of a gardener who boiled water
over an open fire in the garden and bent his corn-
stalks over so the still-attached ears dipped into the
boiling water. The corn was picked *after* it was
cooked.

How sweet is How Sweet It Is? I cooked some
ears picked forty-eight hours earlier and my kids
said it was the best corn they'd ever had.

People think that putting corn in the refriger-
ator keeps it sweet and fresh, but I think the cold
encourages the change from sugar to starch, so we
keep our fresh sweet corn unhusked at a moderate
temperature.

Field corn, which is used to feed chickens, cows, and pigs, is allowed to dry on the stalk until the moisture content of the kernels gets down to about 8 percent, when it will store without molding. In this part of Pennsylvania, where the valley floors roll on for mile after fertile mile, thousands of acres of field corn stand to dry every fall. The kids call it "Corn City."

Sometimes in the tropical heat of summer, when the corn silk is drying and the sweet corn is ripening, I can feel the deep history of corn, going all the way back to Paleolithic times when early Americans gathered the seeds of teosinte, a perennial wild grass of the remote parts of Mexico, and began the long process of selecting the larger grains for planting. After thousands of years of such selection, the grass grew more kernels per ear, and these kernels clung to the cob instead of easily shattering out like the seeds of wild teosinte. The plant lost its perennial gene and became an annual grass—corn. Since the arrival of the Europeans, corn has further transmogrified into better open-pollinated and hybrid types. The hybrids are so regular that a cornfield of a given type will show hardly any variation in height through a whole field. Corn is business. Corn is wealth. It's as familiar to us as our clothes.

Like Ben Seem, corn is direct, abundant, and passionate about producing good crops. Let the food experts quibble about which is the gourmet's chief delight—caviar, lobster, or perhaps the taste of a ripe peach. I say that for all its commonness, a perfect ear of sweet corn is the best food in the world.

Black
Currants

The true repository of the accumulated wisdom of the world is the family tradition. Marilyn's grandparents came to America from Germany earlier in the century, and we've inherited several traditions from them, including my favorite: black currant syrup.

They'd always known and grown black currants in the Old Country, and they brought a few slips with them to their Pennsylvania property. These grew into a fine patch that Marilyn remembers from her girlhood, a patch that still flourishes for the new crop of great grandchildren.

The first time I ate dinner there, Mom's dessert was a frozen lemon bavarian topped with rich, barely sweet, black currant syrup. I'm not much of a one for desserts. I usually pass them up as too heavy, rich, or sugary. But this one looked tempting. The bavarian was cold and creamy with a light citrus tang, and the black currant syrup was warm and bursting with flavor. Mixed directly on the palate, they worked together. The bavarian smoothed and attenuated the rich flavors of the syrup, thinning them out to reveal their delicate facets. I glanced around the dinner table to see if anyone else knew we were eating an ultimate dessert. To a kid they were preoccupied with their bavarian and syrup. I told Mom that she was a genius, and I've never eaten there again without being served that dessert—a fate I richly appreciate.

Soon after that first dinner, we took home some cuttings from Mom's currant bushes and started them in a small nursery patch I tilled up in our field. There they stayed for three years while we planted the orchard and laid out our first large vegetable garden. In the third year we decided to plant the currants along the back of the garden as a hedge. The next spring, before they broke dormancy, I dug them up with big root balls and transplanted them into two rows of eight bushes each in the improved soil at the back of the garden. They were still little bushes in the fourth year. Late that fall I spread horse manure on the ground over their roots, mulched the whole bed with newspapers, and covered it with sawdust to reduce future weed competition. In the fifth year the bushes doubled in size and bore a large crop of big berries. They've matured into a thicket of black currants and have borne huge and regular crops ever since. I cut out wood that's four or five years old. Three-year-old wood seems to have the best and most berries.

Ripe black currants carry a musky flavor that's an acquired taste; even so, when they're hot from the late June sun, they taste both sweet and tart, showing that they have high levels of fruit sugar and acid, and I think they're absolutely delicious. While we eat a few out of hand, most go into a crock with a little sugar and vodka to make cassis. Others are boiled down to syrup, sweetened just a little, and canned, the way Mom does it.

The cassis is for gifts and to mix with our home-made chardonnay when we want to drink kir. The canned syrup is for lemon bavarians or other dishes calling for a fruit syrup. For instance, one of our other favorites is to cover a duckling with orange slices, then a cloth, and baste it with currant syrup. We remove the cloth and slices near the end of cooking and glaze the duckling with the syrup as it's browning. Finally, we reduce some of the syrup to a thick sauce and pour it over the sliced duckling to serve. But if that kind of dish is too much work, you can just pour some syrup on plain old vanilla ice cream. This syrup is a find.

Not long ago we spent a summer afternoon hosting some of Marilyn's relatives who were visiting from Germany. Marlene was about Marilyn's age, a second cousin with a bit of the family resemblance. As we showed them our garden, the relatives began to nod and speak in rapid-fire German when they spied the black currants. "*Johannesbeeren*," one of the group told me, "St. John's Berries." They knew all about the fruit and its wonderful syrup. Back home, they probably knew the very bushes that Mom had cut many years before when she took cuttings to America. Our bushes were cuttings from those cuttings, thriving here in the fertile soils of the New World.

I felt a familial warmth toward this group. Like the black currants, they were related, one branch of the family doing well in America, another thriving back home in Germany.

Currant syrup is a family tradition on both sides of the Atlantic. Home, for this family, is where the black currants are.

Tick Trefoil

*W*hile Nature is innocent in general, she can be devilishly clever in particular. My orchard right now has a bad case of tick trefoil. The weed didn't wait for an invitation. It used me and my habits for its own ends, and has successfully taken over.

Tick trefoils (*Desmodium canadense*), also called beggar ticks, are the little green or brown triangles that stick in neat rows on your pants when you walk through a field of them from late July through September. If you try to rub them off your clothes, they grind tighter into the fabric. They have to be scraped off, and since each triangle is weakly segmented to the next, they break off one by one. You never see them while you're walking. They just appear all over your jeans out of nowhere.

I'm fond of walking around in my orchard, checking out the trees, inspecting the fruit, looking for insect damage, just enjoying the place. Tick trefoil is a recent accoutrement of our place, and the first plant here must have rubbed its ticks in glee when it saw the guy forever walking around the orchard. I'm sure now that I must have stopped and scraped off that plant's seeds under the big Smokehouse apple, for the next year they surrounded the tree. Since I frequently visited the apple tree to pick fruit, wading through the tick trefoil to get there, I must have spread the little beggars everywhere.

Now I understand the plant's tactics: Tiny barbed grappling hooks on thousands of minute hairs cover each triangle; little pirates boarding a dog, a deer, or a human for a ride to an uncontested spot. And I see its strategy: It's looking for some oblivious bozo just like me who walks around in its traps and spreads its seeds all over creation.

But this is why God gave me a brain. I'm human and I'm supposed to be more intelligent than other animals, let alone the plants. Yet tick trefoil outsmarted me, at least for a few years. I suppose that I could refuse to go into the orchard until it gets so thick it crowds itself out, but I'd outsmart myself at the same time. The right answer is the tough one: Keep the field mowed low until the beggar ticks die out. If I discover its tricks, I won't spread its ticks.

What makes me curious is how plants can have tricks that outwit supposedly clever creatures like me. These tricks aren't confined to desmodium. Burdock, sticktights, cockleburs, and other, similar seeds have structures that are hooked or barbed— designed to stick in hair and especially in shoelaces.

Tick trefoil is a simple nuisance weed, hardly central to my gardening efforts, and yet look how elaborate a plan it has laid to catch me, and what's more sobering, how well it has succeeded. Lures and traps lurk in other plants, too. We are held to the rose by the nose and to the raspberry by the tongue. Coffee addicts us. Tobacco attacks us. The poppy sets us dreaming. Wheat holds us by our need to eat.

We use the plants, but seldom stop to think that the plants may be in equal measure using us.

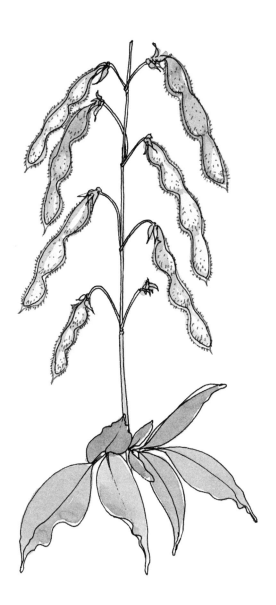

Lamb's-Quarters

*A*fter some calculation, the conservative estimate is that I've pulled over 150,000 lamb's-quarters (*Chenopodium alba*) from our gardens over twelve years here. I must have pulled a thousand today.

It doesn't help to know that they're a nutritious potherb. They invade all my gardens and produce a profusion of seedlings from April to July. Most weeds, like most insects, flowers, and other garden phenomena, have a limited season—from two to six weeks—to do their thing, then disappear. Lamb's-quarters, however, seems to have lost its seasonal limits. I find seedlings all through the growing season. Early cultivation in a problem area may destroy most of the weeds—the wild carrot, for one, will not grow back—but it won't get rid of lamb's-quarters. This weed uses any bare spot to pack in a few more individuals. If the soil is warm, these will explode from seedlings to full-blown weeds in two weeks.

Some patches of lamb's-quarters are stunted, their leaves covered with purple, mottled spots. I suspect a virus is helping me keep down these weeds, but its effect on the overall onslaught of

lamb's-quarters is negligible. Marilyn and I have to
hoe, mow, and hand-pull them. Besides their being a
nuisance in the garden, our son is allergic to their
pollen—a great added incentive for keeping after
them.

No gardener needs to be reminded that weeding
is tedious work. But the necessity to weed has forced
me to adopt an attitude that helps alleviate the tedium. I became a loyal weeder.

Loyal weeding starts with the understanding
that tedium comes from wanting to be somewhere
else, doing something other than weeding. The
weeder becomes bored and restless, dreams of the
hammock, or a loll on the beach. Weeding soon becomes an intolerable chore. The trick is to *want* to
weed, to *love* to weed, to be satisfied with the very
small limits of the weeder's world. Great paintings
have been done on very small canvases, and once the
weeder accepts the narrow confines of the task,
great things can be accomplished. Now the weeder
can lose himself in the work. When the whole heart
is given, there can be no tedium.

Losing oneself in the job of weeding requires
concentration. The constant jibbering of the mind
ceases. The focus narrows. Desire is condensed to
the single-minded purpose at hand. Thus weeding
consumes the loyal weeder the way a sport like
racquetball consumes an expert player.

With the attention focused on the weed patch,
the weeder becomes aware of the several levels of
weeds. First the large weeds are pulled, revealing
much smaller weeds. When these are pulled, the

weeder sees an even more miniscule forest of coty-
ledonous seedlings just emerging. Only the loyal
weeder gets all of these.

Lamb's-quarters looks innocent enough in the
seedling stage, with two bright, apple green blades
preceding the first true leaves. But quickly the stem
elongates, putting out leaves in the rough shape of
the foot of a waterfowl, hence one of its common
names, goosefoot.

Soon the flower structures appear, popping
open thousands of tiny round flowers. Massive seed
heads follow—an infinite production of indestructi-
ble seeds so small that a half dozen might cover the
period on the end of this sentence.

Lamb's-quarters has an unusual ability to
bloom and set seed under conditions that would dis-
courage most weeds. In areas where I cut weeds
down to 6 inches or so with my scythe, most plants
lose their ability to bloom. But lamb's-quarters hun-
kers down and produces flowers in the lower leaf
axils, slipping under the scythe blade and perpetu-
ating itself.

Once lamb's-quarters sets seed, it's too late to
do much about it. It sheds its seeds freely, unlike the
many weeds that hold their seeds more tightly. Cutting down a plant with ripe seed means you'll be
sowing seed with every bouncy step out of the garden.

Is it any wonder that lamb's-quarters is such a
successful plant? It has all the angles figured. Except one. It didn't count on a loyal weeder.

Potatoes

*P*oet and essayist Wendell Berry dropped by the *Organic Gardening* office one day to show slides of his trip to Peru. At the high, remote elevations of the Andes, Wendell found the descendants of the Incas farming potatoes in patches so steep that if the farmer loses his balance, he can tumble thousands of feet down the mountainside.

The photographs of hundreds of worked plots bordered by stone walls on high mountain faces were visually compelling, as if the gods had laid a tracery on the mountaintops.

Peruvian farmers grow over 200 kinds of potatoes, from chunky blue ones to little brown balls, from light-skinned ones and dark-skinned ones to red ones. Since potatoes form most of the people's diet, they have uses for and firsthand knowledge about each kind. Where we would know the difference between a plum, a grape, and a cherry, the farmers of Peru know similar if more subtle differences between types of potatoes. One kind, for instance, is put in a bag and soaked in a stream, then trod upon in the flowing water until a starchy paste remains. This paste is freeze-dried by the cold, dry air of the high mountains and used in a variety of ways.

But in America a potato is just a potato. Sometimes you can find some variety—a bag of Russets, small red early potatoes, big Idaho bakers, Maine all-purpose potatoes—but compared to the dozens of kinds grown by the Andean farmers, there's not much variation at all.

After seeing Wendell's slides, Marilyn and I felt a great desire to plant some potatoes. We acquired seed potatoes from various sources, and one year we grew blue potatoes, Kennebecs, German fingerlings, and some small individuals from the bottom of a bag of commercial bakers.

We were lucky. The weather was perfect that year for potatoes, and all our patches produced. Marilyn liked the blue potatoes best—when fresh, they have a blackish purple skin and a light midnight blue flesh. I found them a bit watery and crumbly when baked. My favorites were the German fingerlings—little spuds the size of small sausages. They're a light yellowish beige when fresh, with a cream-colored flesh, and they are smooth and firm when cooked. The Kennebecs and commercial potatoes grew well and produced representative tubers, which I felt ranked between the blue and fingerling varieties in quality. In all cases, I discovered that potatoes fresh from the ground have a certain something extra on the palate.

When uncovering a hill of any kind of potato, I'm always thrilled when a big specimen comes to light. Small ones disappoint me. My reaction must be the same as that of the millions of people who've grown potatoes through the years. When you're talking about potatoes, bigger usually means better. You would think that potatoes would have reached the size sold commercially today pretty early on in their development, but the fact is that most were the size of eggs until Luther Burbank developed his famous large potato in the late nineteenth century. Luther was a lad of fifteen when he spied in his mother's garden some potato plants that had flowered and were dangling ripe seed balls.

Because people for centuries have propagated potato by planting whole spuds or cut eye pieces, genetic variation through cross-pollination was kept to a minimum. A small potato grows a plant genetically identical to its mother plant, but a potato seed, produced from a flower pollinated by another potato, might carry a new arrangement of genes and surprising new characteristics.

Burbank gathered twenty-five seeds from his mother's plant and planted them in the garden, just because he was curious to see what would happen. Most of the plants turned out to be scrawny hybrids, but one seed produced a plant that grew the biggest potatoes Luther had ever seen, or, in fact, anyone had ever seen. Within a few years, Luther Burbank's large russet potatoes—which we still eat today— had revolutionized the potato industry, ended the potato famine in Ireland, and upped profits for farmers. Burbank went on to spend his life experimenting with plants, exploring the hidden treasures of his plants' genes, and delivering to the world a list of new and useful plants that would fill a book.

All the types of potatoes grown in the Andes exist in the genes of modern potatoes, although they remain for the most part unexpressed. The history of the plant is genetically coded and filed away in the vegetable equivalent of a memory. The potato has adapted itself to varying conditions over its long history, and all of these adaptations are stored in this memory, waiting for changing environmental conditions to call them forth. That's how plants— and animals—can adapt in just a few generations to rapidly changing environments. For instance, perhaps millions of years ago a plant had made an adaptation to increasing cold. If the modern plant's environment turns cold, that old adaptation will eventually emerge and save the species.

One day late in the year that we grew all the potatoes, my friend Jim and I decided to cook dinner, so the rest of our families went out while we worked for hours in the kitchen. When they came home, we'd prepared a real feast comprised of eleven different potato dishes. We had hash browns, french fries, home fries, mashed potatoes, parsley browned potatoes, au gratin, julienne, baked, boiled, potato pancakes, and potatoes raw as a salad. And it was a truly delicious meal. At the end of it, nibbling my last raw potato stick, I knew how the Andean farmers felt about their 200 kinds of spuds. Unlike them, though, I didn't eat a potato again for a week.

White Oak

*T*he forest around our house is dominated by tulip poplar and black birch, and therein lies a great deal of the history of the land. According to references on the natural history of this region (41°N. latitude; 1,150 ft. above sea level), oaks should predominate, but only a few white oaks (*Quercus alba*) and a handful of other oaks grow in the forest, and these are small. A hundred years ago, the references say, American chestnut and white oak shared the throne as the giants of these woods, but I don't believe it. I'll bet that white oaks were as hard to find then as they are now. Yet this is prime white oak territory. So where are the oaks? The answer lies in economic history.

Over the centuries, white oak has always been prized. The wood is very tough and useful where strength is important, such as for wagon tongues and chair rockers. It's also a beautiful, light wood with interesting grain. White oak had many uses, from barn beams to high-quality firewood, from the best barrels to a source of tannin for curing hides. Needless to say, white oaks started disappearing quickly after the Europeans got here.

Five hundred years ago, before the Europeans, I'm sure this land was covered with white oak and chestnut. The annual shower of nuts from both trees must have supported an abundance of wildlife and made game plentiful for the Indians. Now, if a white oak raises its head too high, it's sure to be cut down.

In place of oak, we find tulip poplar and black birch. They were left standing when the oak, maple, hickory, and other more useful woods were selected out.

We've already seen why tulip poplars predominate, but why do we have so much black birch? Again, because of human activity. Since Colonial days, this part of the country has been a source of birch oil, which is used to flavor soft drinks.

A man lived here before we came, not in our stone house, but in a cabin halfway out our lane. Old Milt Rohrbach—that was the man's name—was a birch cutter; he lashed saplings of black birch into bundles which he'd carry to the birch distillery two miles east in a high vale called The Gap.

When you cut birch saplings, the roots send up two or three new shoots from every cut. Thus, the more that Milt Rohrbach cut, the more there was. Over the years, he turned most of this hillside into a birch forest. Since he has been gone, a richer mix of trees is growing back, but most are not yet full-sized.

Tulip poplar and black birch. My tenure here has witnessed the peak of their ascendancy. I suspect that from now on, this hillside will begin to revert to its rightful owner—the white oak.

A local fellow we once met told us that white oak is a magical plant. He said that to show its magical nature, it produces a five-pointed star in the center of its limbs, which one can see if a cut is made across a limb. I've often thought about that when looking at young white oaks, but I've never actually cut a limb and verified the tale.

Yet I feel something special when I'm near a white oak, especially a full-grown one. There was such a tree growing all alone in a field near my dad's house, where I grew up. Calling that tree "mighty" doesn't do it justice. The trunk must have been 6 feet in diameter and its major limbs were bigger than the trunks of most full-grown trees.

I went to that tree often when I was a boy, full of confusion and wonder and promise. In the shade of its huge arms, I felt a calm and stability, like being with a grandfather whose years are so many they stretch beyond my ability to grasp them.

I knew that the tree must have endured much over its centuries. Ice storms came to periodically break off large limbs. Thunderstorms must have often loaded their shotguns with hail and let the tree have it. Birds and animals must have lived out their small triumphs and tragedies in its branches. But the oak is steadfast. Today's torments always end. Limbs can mend and new leaves will sprout.

When I need to feel strong, I close my eyes and become that old oak. I am rooted with such mammoth strength that no vicissitude can break me. I am calm and silent at the core. And I bathe and grow in the pleasant light that falls from the sun that crosses my heaven.

Apricots

When the kids were tots, we planted two apricot trees for them, a Sungold and a Moongold. The next year the trees were strong little saplings, but while mowing the field with a sickle-bar mower, I inadvertently cut off the Moongold. I made a mental note to order another one from the nursery.

The note got lost on my mental desk. In fact, I'd completely forgotten about the sliced-off apricot when, making my rounds in the orchard, I noticed the stump had pushed up four shoots. I let them all grow that year to strengthen the roots, but the next spring I cut away three and left the fourth to grow into a new trunk.

Within two years the reborn Moongold caught up with the undisturbed Sungold tree, and now, eight years later, it's twice the Sungold's size. At first I thought perhaps I'd cut off the grafted part, and the more vigorous rootstock was sending up shoots. But the shoots arose above the graft knob. For some reason, the damaged tree had come roaring back.

I'd seen the same thing happen with a young grapevine that was lopped off at ground level during dormancy. In the spring, it sent out one huge cane that bolted for the top of the trellis and made it there before the less vigorous canes from its undamaged siblings. In fact, an axiom of grape pruning holds that the more severely the vine is pruned, the more vigorously next season's shoots will grow. When the vine is pruned very severely, it responds with big bull canes.

The Moongold apricot proved that this effect extended beyond grapes, and I think it even goes deep into human experience, where adversity is the fire in which strength is forged. Childhood poverty has goaded many people to great achievements, and those who've climbed the farthest to reach the top relish it the most. Illness or injury has been responsible for more than one athletic champion who has exercised his or her way back to health and then beyond. Creativity, too, can be stimulated by illness, as poet Samuel Taylor Coleridge maintained. Recuperation, he thought, was a time when things that were shaken loose by illness came back together in new ways, and new insights were gained.

I see in my own life that times of darkest trouble have forced the greatest changes upon me. I've always emerged into calmer waters to find life sweeter, surprised at how much I've grown.

During daylight hours, plants struggle with the business of the day, but when the sun goes down and the leaves close, in the quiet of the night, their growth takes place. Growth always happens unseen and can only be recognized in retrospect, whether in apricot trees or our hearts.

Because the Moongold has grown so much bigger than its companion, it produces many more apricots.

We can't always count on having fruit, however. These trees have a very early blooming habit: the first part of April around here. Our last frost date is May 10, which means that frost is certainly a possibility while the apricots are blooming. Once the blossoms set fruit, light frosts won't harm the young 'cots. Our trees set fruit only about three out of every five years; in the other two we're disappointed by frost.

Of course, the disappointment only increases our anticipation of next year's crop and adds an indefinable sweetness to it. Once again a hardship has brought forth its reward.

Bottle
Gentian

*T*he bottle gentian (*Gentiana andrewsii*) is finicky about the conditions it prefers—lots of moisture, but not too much; lots of light, but not too much; lots of humus in the soil, but not too much. It was no terrific surprise, therefore, that our bottle gentians, after a few years of indifferent growth, finally died out, even though we gave them what we thought were ideal growing conditions.

That's why I felt a twinge of resentment recently when I found a beautiful stand of bottle gentians growing wild in a rough, rank, weedy ditch. A more unlikely spot for these delicate plants could hardly be imagined, although the luminous blue tubes of the gentian flowers rescued the place from abject ugliness.

They won't grow for me, but they'll grow fine in a dirty ditch. Most garden plants are adaptable and easy, but bottle gentians are standoffish and hard to please. Because of this, they're relatively rare in the wild, and even rarer in gardens.

Even the plants' flowers are reluctant to open. A blossom remains closed until a bee, driven wild by the enticement of the fragrant nectar within, pries apart the tips of the petals and crawls inside.

No daytime pollinator like a bee would dare enter a dark interior where a spider might be lurking. The gentian, therefore, has drained most of the blue coloring from the base of its petals, creating translucent panels that flood the interior of the flower with an unearthly bluish light. I have peered into these chambers, and it's then that I wish I could climb inside like a bee, drink a cup of the floral nectar, and bathe heart and soul in the healing blue glow.

Gentians bloom late, starting in August and continuing well into October, shyly saving their flowers until the more garish displays of high summer are finished.

What value does the bottle gentian find in all this modesty? Does playing hard to get maximize its chances of survival in some way? Is its sweet sip really the Chateau Lafite of nectars, worth the extra effort?

By the price it exacts from the bees to reach its nectaries, the bottle gentian discourages all but the most dedicated pollinators, the ones with a taste for quality. In human affairs, people drink an enormous amount of wine worldwide each year, almost all of it ordinary. Only those willing to part with the cash that represents the fruit of their labors get to taste the Lafites and Romanee-Contis. The choice vintages, like the nectars of bottle gentians, are rare.

In such an infinite profusion of life as grows in

the countryside, there must be one species that by its own devices makes itself precious and therefore sought out by its devotees.

My long-departed bottle gentians become ever more precious to me. Not only are they physically gone, even their memories are gathering the dust that settles over time and finally buries the past beyond recall.

Broccoli

J had an inkling that there was something unusual about broccoli when our daughter, Chandra,
who was two at the time, grew a gargantuan specimen with the aid of her rubber Mickey Mouse.

She and her brother Shane, who was four that
year, planted their broccoli seedlings alongside a
row of four plants that Marilyn and I set out. When
Chandra was finished patting down the earth and
watering her young plant, she set her rubber Mickey
under its leaves; there he stayed while the broccoli
grew to cover the area with masses of large, blue-
green leaves.

All our plants were productive but not remarkable in size—except for Chandra's. Her plant produced a head 18 inches across, compared to the 8- to
10-inch heads on the others. We brought out the
camera and posed Chandra, in sundress and red ban-
danna, by her masterpiece.

We laughed at the developed print. There in the
picture, along with Chandra and the big broccoli,
was the face of Mickey Mouse peering out from between two wide leaves. We'd forgotten he was there.

I reasoned that broccoli responded to TLC—even (and maybe especially) infantile TLC. During the next winter I thought about what we could do for the broccoli that it might like, and decided that it would probably like the stable straw from the goat pen. Full of goat droppings and soaked with urine, the straw would give the plants a drink of manure tea every time it rained. The following spring we placed a glass marble on the ground next to each seedling as a gift, then mulched them all with the stable straw.

Evidently my reasoning was correct. We grew the biggest heads we'd ever seen on several of the plants, and almost all of them produced whoppers.

TLC for the broccoli also meant keeping cabbage worms off the plants with a spray of *Bacillus thuringiensis*, a bacterial disease that affects caterpillars. And it meant keeping down the weeds.

Broccoli wants to do well for the gardener: It's bred for big production. But too often it's planted in poor soil, not given enough water, neglected in the weeds, and ignored while cabbage worms and loopers chew it to pieces.

Most years since then, we've grown great crops of broccoli, refining our technique as we go. We now set out the started plants in mid-April to give them an early start. They make harvestable heads before the Fourth of July, before the cabbage worms get impossible. I pull each plant after taking the main head, rather than letting them grow small, secondary heads. These are inferior because they emerge in August when it's usually hot and dry, the kind of weather that gives the broccoli a heavy cabbagey taste and smell. Pulling the plants early also prevents the cabbage moths from using them as nurseries for their swarming broods of young.

In return for all this special attention, broccoli gives us a fabulously nutritious food. Ounce for ounce among common vegetables, broccoli is the most nutritious food we eat, rich in most vitamins, packed with food energy, and reportedly preventive against disease.

When I pull the plants, I like to break off the main stem and sip the sap that rises to the broken stem from the roots. It's a draft that I seldom get to taste, and never in quantity, but it gives me the greatest feeling of well-being, as if the sap were the essence of the nutritive powers of the plant. Maybe that's broccoli's way of caring for me, tenderly, with love.

*Eulalia
Grass*

*J*went looking in the garden today for the plant that best represents the qualities of an old friend of mine. He's now the president of a successful company, but we go back to college days when he was the president of our fraternity. The same quality that caused our rather ragtag bunch of overgrown boys to elect him house president brought him to the top of his company. He never fought his way into these positions—he rose quietly into them, was asked into them, as if he belonged there.

It was to try to define that quality that I went to the garden. I only knew that the plant I was looking for would occupy a presidential position.

Daylilies skimmed over the drifts of other flowers in bursts of bright yellow, orange, red, burgundy, and raspberry. Was my friend like the daylilies? No. He's far less showy and a lot more efficient. He'd never hold onto his spent blossoms: He's always prepared to cut off any part that doesn't contribute to the whole.

I snooped around, evaluating various trees, shrubs, roses, and even the vegetables. But the blue-collar tomatoes and the odd, pungent parsley weren't like him at all.

Something kept drawing me back to the daylilies, though I knew they weren't the plant I sought. The path in the upper garden is flanked with two exquisite daylilies. One is a deep royal red, the other is the color of black raspberry ice cream. Both types have rich, golden throats. I noticed then that all the daylilies in our gardens, near and far, had open throats, angled upwards, spilling gold into the morning air. Though they sang silently, I could imagine their chorus, sounding off in some realm beyond my senses. The deep reds sang bass. The middle colors sang the alto and tenor parts. And the light lemon and yellows sang soprano.

As I looked at the daylily chorus arrayed across the lower gardens in a gentle arc, I saw for the first time that from the vantage point of the upper garden, the scene focused on the huge, ball-shaped mass of 8-foot-tall eulalia grass in the background. I'd never before noticed how that erupting fountain of long, grassy leaves pulled the picture together.

I knew immediately that the grass was a plant much like my friend. It is one of the biggest, most dominant perennials on the property, one of few that were here when we moved in, and one whose true role was long overlooked through familiarity.

The spray of eulalia grass (*Miscanthus sinensis* 'Gracillimus') is the first part of the property one sees coming down the long driveway. Greeting everyone and presaging horticultural effects to come, it's there in all seasons, including winter, when its brown stalks and skeletal plumes, blown free of fluff by cold winds, persist. I realized that we'd subconsciously built all our gardens around it.

Across the lawn from the grass, for instance, I'd built a semicircular stone wall which now has tiers of flowers rising above it. Now I could see the eulalia grass conducting the flowers' golden-throated choruses. Like any conductor, it's easy to overlook, but nevertheless central to the performance of the composition. Secretly and in hidden ways it has been selecting the score, orchestrating the music, and pulling the voices together in harmony.

That hidden, yet potent, power is exactly the quality shown by my friend over the years. He's a natural conductor. He accomplishes his work behind the scenes, leaving the role of featured singer to someone else.

But what, I wondered, was the source of the power that naturally leads the way for others? I walked down to the eulalia grass for a closer look. If this plant were truly representative of my friend, then I'd find the answer. At this time of year, mid-July, the grass blades are nearly full-grown, but the new plumes haven't yet emerged. The dried bones of last year's plumes are still there, however, held another 2 or 3 feet above the tall, straplike leaves.

Each grass blade, I noticed, has a white stripe down the center. White is the color of honesty and fairness. The leaves seemed to say that my friend is honest at the core, thus inspiring trust. The president of a company is entrusted with the well-being of that company. The board of directors would not choose someone they couldn't trust implicitly.

The dried plumes looked like shepherds' crooks. That completed the picture for me: The shepherd has ever been the symbol for a caring individual entrusted with the welfare and safety of a flock. To lead that way is really to serve, for the shepherd keeps the interests of the flock foremost when making decisions.

Now I know my friend's secret. In truth, the daylilies told me, or rather, they silently sang the answer into the high reaches of my understanding.

Avocados

*A*lmost everyone has sprouted an avocado pit and grown it into an avocado (*Persea americana*). Some years ago it seemed that every windowsill in America was issued an egg-shaped seed, which was spoked with toothpicks and set into a jar of water to wet its bottom. Sometimes roots would grow and a little stem would hold a few leaves aloft, but the plants rarely lasted long.

One of the first things Marilyn and I ever planted was one of those avocado seeds. During our first spring together it grew leaves and roots in its jar on a sunny windowsill. We transplanted it to a pot for the summer and brought it into the house in the fall. Dry August and September weather had left the plant weak and tattered. At the time, we were renting a big, old, drafty farmhouse—uninsulated—and heating it with two balky old coal stoves. When the stoves burned low, we'd freeze; when they burned bright, we'd roast.

The cold days of late fall and winter indoors didn't agree with the avocado. We eventually gave it up for dead and put it out on the front porch in January. That winter turned out to be a mild one, and temperatures seldom got below the mid-twenties at night. The leafless green stem froze and turned black nevertheless. For the balance of the winter and the following spring, a pot with a dead stick decorated our crumbling front porch.

That February, the landlady announced that we had to move—her nephew wanted to live in the house. So in spring we moved to our current prop-

erty, about 10 miles north and 600 feet higher in elevation than the old farmhouse. On our last trip back to pick up a few odds and ends from the old place, we noticed that the base of the dead avocado stick was trying to put out some leaves, but these were small and thirsty-looking. We threw the pot in the truck and brought it here. After repotting and a good watering, the plant revived and put out a bundle of leaves, obviously overjoyed to be rescued.

For the next three years, the avocado plant took its chances outside in summer and spent the winters inside with inadequate light. Each spring the plant looked like it was about to give up the ghost, but it always perked up and put out new growth when moved outside.

Then we installed the big skylight in our roof. The avocado now had plenty of light in both summer and winter. The first full winter under the skylight it was so delighted that it actually bloomed—one little blossom that was later picked off by a well-meaning friend who wanted to "show it" to us.

The plant has never bloomed again, but it has kept growing, and we've repotted it into bigger pots several times. It's now in a huge clay pot that holds 10 gallons of soil and takes two people to lift. The topmost leaves reach nearly 9 feet above the ground.

I can count its branches (46) and leaves (517) because I'm writing this in its shade, on the deck behind the house, where it vacations for the summer. In the winter it sits under the skylight, the pot on the second floor and its upper branches playing among the tropical vegetation that hangs just under the skylight's dome. The avocado has never looked healthier, and the lower part of the trunk has developed true avocado tree bark instead of the green alligator skin typical of young wood.

The leaves seem to be covered with microscopic droplets of oil, which makes them very glossy. Sunlight makes them glisten with myriads of prismatic red and green points in intricate patterns.

The avocado has been with us from the beginning. It has been ignored. It has been hung with Christmas ornaments. Our kids have sheltered, even in the dead of winter, under its branches. We think of it as family—the first fruit of a fruitful relationship and a living reminder of a time when love was new.

Gooseberries

*T*he most painful chore of the gardening year may be the annual pruning of the gooseberry patch.

The wood and twigs on our variety, which we took as cuttings from Marilyn's grandmother's garden, bristle with long, hard, sharp thorns. They prick the skin with a horrible intensity and a deep ache that accompanies the quick pain of the puncture. One doesn't expect such a luscious, lovely plant to attack the forearms and hands so viciously.

I'm glad that I've come to this chore at a mature stage of my life, and the gooseberries ought to be relieved, too. When I was a tot and hurt myself, my mom soothed my tears by feigning anger at whatever I'd stumbled over or bumped into, and would hit it and speak sharply to it. I suppose I learned then to get angry at whatever hurt me, whether the hurt was fancied or real, whether it was from a rock, plant, bee, or another person. If I'd pruned gooseberries as a young man, I probably would have gotten even with their painful bites by hacking them down.

To overcome this problem, I had to learn that the hurts I suffered were usually my own fault—I stubbed my own toe, I stuck my arm in the gooseberries, I imposed demands on those around me, then turned resentful and angry when they fell short of meeting those demands.

If the hurt wasn't my fault, but was a real wrong done to me, I had to learn to see that the problem was not mine, but lay coiled instead in the heart of the person who was callous or vindictive enough to cause me pain. This attitude, I discovered, carries with it the impetus to do something to help such a person.

I found out that help doesn't mean rescuing someone from their iniquity or giving them a program for righteous living. It means approaching them gingerly so that, despite their flaws, you can still be their friend. Flawed people, which includes just about all of us, need friends, too.

I get the chance to practice what I preach when I give the gooseberries their annual pruning. With gooseberries, as with their cousins, the red and black currants, I leave the younger stems, four years old or less, and take out the older stems. I first approached this job with thick gloves and a padded jacket, but pruning gooseberries is a delicate task, taking close, careful work to cut out the dead and old wood and leave just the best fruiting wood. The gloves and jacket were too bulky to give me the freedom I needed to do the job properly, so within a few years I stopped using them.

Now I prune the gooseberries in a T-shirt. This has proved to be the best way by far, for it forces me to be deliberate and very gentle. If I concentrate and carefully find places to grasp the stems with thumb and forefinger, I can avoid the whorls of thorns at each node and prune the whole patch without getting stuck.

The gooseberries are entitled to their thorns. My job, if I want to keep them as productive friends, is to accept them as they are and not get entangled in their bitter embrace. They, in turn, appreciate the velvet touch. The more years I perform this task, the more beautiful the bushes look after pruning and the more fruitful they grow. This year, particularly, the fruit hangs so heavily that it weighs down the branches. The blue jays have been eating lots of it and so have we.

The bushes remain just as thorny as ever, but now I work them without a problem, and as a result am inundated with fruit.

Sage

$\mathcal{B}$ecause of an expectation of a raise and a promotion that didn't materialize, my friend feels his fortunes reversed, and he has lost faith in himself. It shows in his bitterness and resentment toward the people who passed him over and the people who surpassed him for the job.

I've commiserated with him. I've chewed him out for having such expectations in the first place. And I've advised him to drop the hostility and get on with doing a good job, which is the only action he can take that will get him the recognition he wants.

None of it has worked. He's cheerful until the subject of his work comes up. Then the familiar litany of complaints begins. If I were wiser and more sage, perhaps I could gain a useful insight into his problem and suggest a foothold he could use to climb out of the pit he has dug for himself.

Sage was known in ancient times as a plant that increases wisdom and restores lost youth. Those are heavy claims, and I'm in need of a little wisdom to help my friend, so I've decided to visit the garden and eat a couple of leaves of our purple sage (*Salvia purpurea*). We can have an on-the-spot test of sage's purported powers, right here and now.

Since writing the previous sentence, I've gone to the garden and plucked two young leaves from the purple sage. Their pebbley surface and slightly medicinal, goaty smell brought a vision of Mediterranean shores to mind, the hills dotted with sage bushes and the sea stretching flat away to the horizon. I thought of the thousands of years and the many generations of ancients who must have known this smell and hoped for wisdom from eating the leaves or drinking tea from the plant. I remembered how, in past years, I'd take some homegrown dried sage leaves from the herb jar and rub them to a woolly powder between my palms, then lace the Thanksgiving turkey stuffing with it. And I looked at the plant with an eye to its family heritage—it not only produced a culinary and medicinal herb, but also developed cousins with beautiful red, white, and blue annual and perennial flowers. As I chewed the leaves, I thought about how sage has developed a remarkable mechanism for insuring pollination. The flowers produce nectar behind a flap of tissue. When a bee's tongue hits this flap, two hinged stamens descend from the roof of the flower and coat the bee's back with pollen.

Now I have finished chewing the sage leaves and have swallowed them. The typewriter sits dumbly before me, waiting for words. And the following line of reasoning does surface in my consciousness:

We can choose to hold a pit full of bitterness in our minds, or we can choose to drain it. To get beyond our disappointments we must believe in a benevolent universe. Our job is to feel that benevolence and pass it along to those around us.

To believe in the essential goodness of the universe when we are turning on the spit of disappointment and anger is difficult. That's when we need to remember that if we change our minds, we change the world.

I won't tell this to my friend. But today I learned that I've got to get some sage tea into him as soon as possible. It could help him change his mind.

Tomatoes

*T*omato culture is a dirty job, but someone's got to do it. There's precious little romance in the tomato, despite its old moniker of "love apple." But there is a feature of the tomato that endears it to the hearts of gardeners everywhere. Despite our best efforts at growing it wrong, it will overwhelm us with fruit if given half a chance.

Nothing wows visitors to the garden like a fine stand of tomatoes. Tomatoes are the roses of the vegetable world: common but always impressive. Because a good tomato patch is the central ornament of the vegetable garden, I can think of no higher praise for this plant than to grow it well. In a dozen years of growing tomatoes, I've distilled what I've learned to the following:

Some tomatoes, like the "Boys" (Big Boy, Better Boy, Wonder Boy, Ultra Boy) are indeterminate. That means their shoots keep elongating through the growing season, throwing out clusters of tomato flowers as they grow. The "Girls," on the other hand, are often determinate. That means that they put out a single crop of tomatoes, then retire for the season. For a home gardener, the indeterminate kinds keep fruit coming in late summer and are usually preferred, although many gardeners swear by determinate kinds. Market gardeners find that determinate tomatoes ripen a single crop over a relatively short period and so are better for farm-oriented harvesting.

An important, if neglected, tomato-growing technique is suckering. Shoots that arise in the leaf axils should be pinched off to keep the plants' energy flowing to the places where the tomatoes are growing.

Be wary of tomatoes that aren't marked VFN in the catalogs. VFN means they're resistant to verticillium and fusarium wilts, as well as the soil-dwelling, wormlike pests called nematodes. I've grown wilt-susceptible varieties and, sure enough, just when they're going great, they suddenly wilt and come crashing down in a limp mass.

It's no favor to the tomatoes to plant them in soil enriched with manure or to give them lots of fish emulsion. Too much nitrogen in these fertilizers causes tomatoes to create vegetative growth at the expense of reproductive growth. Ordinary garden soil enriched with finished compost will be fine. In fact, the soil may not even need to be enriched. Tomatoes planted in holes dug in the lawn outperformed those planted anywhere else, including mulched garden soil, in an experimental trial at the Rodale Research Center a few years ago.

If the weather turns cold when the tomatoes are flowering, you'll see them drop their blossoms like tiny yellow parachutes. When the weather warms up, new blossoms will hang on to set fruit.

Tomatoes do demand water. If conditions turn droughty for even a short time when the tomatoes are making fruit, you'll see blossom end rot develop—brown, mushy, decayed spots at the blossom end of the fruit. Tomatoes fruit best in good garden soil with steady, adequate moisture. That means serious tomato growers will think about installing drip irrigation in the form of a hose with emitters or a soaker hose.

If you find an occasional tomato hornworm on your plants, don't kill it, especially if it has little white dots on its back. Those dots are the eggs of a parasitic wasp, and they will hatch into a brood that kills the worm they're attached to. Hornworms need management only if they are destroying plants.

When choosing tomato seedlings at the market in spring, pick those that are young, thrifty, and carry no more than a few small green fruits, if any fruit at all. Bigger, lusher plants with large green fruits carry too much foliage and fruit aloft for newly transplanted roots to service, and they usually get set back so far by transplanting that they never catch up to younger plants.

When starting tomato seed in flats, figure on transplanting them twice before putting them outside for the summer season. Transplant them to individual pots when they get about 2 inches high and set them at least as deep as they grew, if not a little deeper. Handle them by the leaves, not the stem. A fork is a good tool to use for separating the seedlings from the flat. When the plants get 4 to 6 inches tall, transplant them to a larger pot. Pinch off some of each plant's bottom leaves so you can bury more of the stem in the new pot. The buried tomato stem will put out new roots, which will give the plants more grow power when they reach the garden.

Unless you have a sunny skylight or glassed sunroom, tomato seedlings will do best under two full-spectrum fluorescent tubes (grow-lights) hung over the seedlings by chains that can be drawn up. Keep the lights close to the young plants, moving them up as the plants grow. Seedlings do best where the air temperature is about 60 to 65 degrees.

Although tomatoes need steady moisture outside in the garden, it's a good idea to keep the potted seedlings a little dry to keep luxuriant growth down, and to encourage the new roots to elongate as they search for water. But although you go light on the water, don't ever let the plants wilt.

Acclimate your young plants to the outside world slowly, a few hours the first day, a few more the second day, during all the daylight hours the third day, until 8 or 9 P.M. on the fourth day, then all night the fifth day, if the night will be relatively warm. After that you can transplant them to the garden, if all frost danger is past.

Tomatoes need to be tied up off the ground. Fruit that touches the ground, even the mulch on top of the soil, rots as it ripens. For best results, use a tomato cage—heavy gauge wire in a wide, 5-inch mesh that's sold as swimming pool reinforcing wire at any pool materials supplier. Eight feet of this mesh curls into a cylinder about 2⅛ feet in diameter.

The cylinder is placed over the young plant, and as the plant grows, the shoots can be tied to the wires and easily positioned. Fruit hanging inside the wire is easily reached. Anchor the cylinder to the ground with tent pegs or rocks, as summer winds could blow it over and rip out the plant roots.

When the weather cools in September, expect a lot of cracked, imperfect fruit. Select perfect green fruit of good size to wrap in newspaper and place in a cool, dark attic for ripening over the next month or so. Check these often for spoilage.

Try two or three kinds of tomatoes at first and determine which you like best. Plant them again in subsequent years, pairing them with new varieties until you find a kind you like even better. Make that your new champion and keep trying new varieties. After a number of years, you'll have found your ulti-mate tomato.

Mine? Ultra Boy for big production, Beefsteak for the best taste, and Sweet 100 for cherry toma-toes.

And there you have my ultimate tribute to the tomato—the distilled techniques of a dozen years. They work, and what works has a particularly sturdy beauty.

Bee Balm

*B*ecause of unique environmental conditions, the Pocono Mountains region of eastern Pennsylvania puts on a glorious flower show each year, featuring profusions of wild flowers that may be rare in other areas. I know of fields full of pearly everlasting. The late spring woods are full of wild azalea, rhododendron, and mountain laurel. And the late summer fields around my boyhood home were purple with bee balm flowers.

When I remember those fields, I'm a thirteen-year-old, carrying my BB-gun, my head full of the heady aroma of the leaves. It's always a hot August day, and the heat and sun vaporize the essential oils produced by this mint family member, creating a scent that hangs at nose level above the plants in the heavy, still air.

My arms are brown from weeks in the summer sun. My body is strangely long. Shocks of hair hang over my eyes, sheepdog fashion, because of my determination to avoid a haircut until school reopens. The fields are humming with the sound of bees working the tapered, tubular flowers that emerge in a crown from the composite seed heads.

Bee balm is aptly named, and each lavender flower head of *Monarda fistulosa*, the wild bee balm's botanical name, contains a busy yellow and black bee, in those fields of my childhood. I used to walk through dense stands of bee balm without fear of the insects, for they're gentle when collecting nectar.

All I need to do now is sniff bee balm's pungent smell to be transported in time and place back to that scene. The aroma is hard to characterize. It has the biting edge of mint, but is not minty. It's vaguely like tea, and history tells us that the American colonists used bee balm for tea when supplies from England dried up after the Boston Tea Party. In many places, the plant is known as Oswego tea, after the Indian tribe who brewed it.

We now grow five kinds of bee balm. *Monarda fistulosa* does well in sun and in poor, shaley soil, such as we had in the Poconos, so its light lavender flowers grace our sunniest garden. Another species, *Monarda didyma*, comes in various colors and prefers a light shade in a rich, moist soil. The area below our deck has those conditions, so we started a few plants of *M. didyma* 'Cambridge Scarlet' there years ago. Just the other day we spotted a hummingbird sipping nectar in the big patch that has naturalized there. He was slipping his curved needle bill into the similarly curved flowers. Our Cambridge Scarlet has spread its rich red crowns all over the area, making the July and August view from the deck dissolve into red dots on a green background.

For the first time this year, Marilyn has established a large, sweet drift of *Monarda didyma* 'Croftway Pink' in the upper garden. This variety carries lovely soft pink crowns. In our garden, they're visited by little grey and black bees that look like flies. The pink and black color scheme also has the power to transport me back, this time to Sister Theresa Claire's seventh grade classroom and the time I wore a pink shirt with a Mr. B collar and a pair of gray and black pegged pants to class. She sent me home.

In the garden just outside my office, the white bee balm, *Monarda didyma* 'Snow White,' is getting ready to bloom. We also have a magenta variety whose name we don't know.

I've made the acquaintance of most of the plants and flowers in our garden only since becoming an adult. As a kid, I wasn't aware of too many plants' names. I didn't, for instance, know the name of the bee balm that surrounded our house and perfumed our air. But I must have had an inkling of its name, for I'm never in those fields without my BB-gun, drowned in the humming of thousands of happy bees.

Sugar
Snap
Peas

*L*et's try to remember the days before sugar snap peas.

That's when pea-growing required some thought, and almost more effort than it was worth. First we had to decide which of the dozens of varieties offered in the catalogs we wanted. It took me years to settle on a first sowing of Alaska Early peas, just to get peas as soon as possible, for nothing beats the fresh green taste of the first ripe peas. They are delicious more for their being the first sweet vegetable of the gardening year than for any inherent quality.

For the main crop of peas I had to experiment, and over the years planted Laxton's Progress, Green Arrow, Lincoln, Progress #9, and several others, without coming to any firm conclusions about which was best. All seemed decent enough, and the crops were big.

All were also the devil to shell out for freezing, but there was no way around the task, and many of our late June hours were spent at the kitchen table, listening to the radio, laboriously squeezing the pods open, and running a thumb down the concave interior of the pods to free the peas. Thus a bushel of pea pods would be reduced to a half gallon of peas.

These had to be blanched in boiling water, then plunged into an ice bath, then tied up in freezer bags and carted off to the freezer.

In the winter, when we'd eat the peas, we'd warm them gently until they were just hot, to preserve their fresh flavor. They tasted okay. Just okay. Certainly they were nothing like garden fresh peas whose full sweetness is intact.

The peas also required trellising. For several years I'd gather dead branches and stick them in the ground for the peas to climb on, but the tall, main crop varieties always outgrew the branches and tumbled all over themselves. So I switched to various arrangements of twine slung between poles. What usually happened was that the weight of full-grown, fully podded vines pulled down most of my bizarre twine creations. I then tried bush peas, figuring to avoid trellising altogether, but I didn't like the way the plants trailed their pods in the mud, or the quality of the peas.

While I (along with many other gardeners) was struggling with peas, out in Idaho plant breeder Calvin Lamborn was perfecting the horticultural introduction of the century—the sugar snap pea. This is the delicacy one eats pod and all, except for the fibrous string that comes off the pod with a quick zip.

I'd always wanted a fully edible pea, and never really cared for the Chinese type called the snow pea, either raw or stir-fried. So the year sugar snaps were introduced, I jumped at the chance to plant them and decided I was going to erect a trellis that would hold up pumpkins if it had to. I drove steel fence posts in the ground, then hung plastic mesh netting from a wire strung through the top holes of the posts.

The sugar snaps came roaring out of the ground, rushed to the top of their trellis, and produced a huge crop of superb, crunchy pods filled with sweet little peas. The ads for the peas said that they were also good for freezing, so we blanched the pods and froze them, figuring to tear off the string when we thawed them in winter. We took out our first bag in October, but found that the pods were mushy and off-tasting. The peas, however, which rolled right out of the soggy pods, were perfect. The pods had evidently protected them from the direct heat of blanching, and when warmed gently, the peas had that elusive, sweet character of fresh peas.

Without a doubt, the introduction of sugar snaps was one of the great improvements in twentieth-century vegetable gardening. I was very satisfied, but also set to musing.

I'd taken peas for granted as entirely useful and perfected, with little room for improvement. I'd never dreamed that someday I'd be able to eat pods and all, right off the vine, and achieve fresh taste in frozen peas. The experience made me think about what other common plants might have in store in the future, when some genius plants-person coaxes them to transcend their current incarnations.

What might roses become, for instance? Perhaps someday they'll be a fruit crop as well as an ornamental. Who knows what might happen to bitter little hawthorn berries if they are bred up to the size of an apple and turn sugary sweet?

And who knows what might happen to people if one day we learn to see our own potentials? Perhaps each one of us, drawing from the infinitude of human potentials, might become something we now only dream about.

Pears

*M*y dad's old Bartlett pear tree produced heavy crops of green pears. They'd finish ripening on the breezeway, turning a golden yellow as the firm flesh melted into sugar. Both the taste and texture of those pears were extraordinary, and word must have gotten out. For the last few years that my dad lived at his home in the Poconos, he never tasted a pear, for thieves came in the night and stole every luscious fruit just when they were ready to pick.

I haven't tasted a pear either, although I planted two Bartletts seven years ago and they are now handsome little trees. They've yet to flower, let alone set fruit. At least I can be confident no thieves will come by.

Of all the fruits planted here, I most wanted the taste of the Bartlett pear, to recapture the flavor I knew as a boy and to pass the experience along to our kids. But so far we've been denied. Each spring I inspect the pear buds for signs of flowers, but in vain.

Orchardists aren't helpless in the face of barren fruit trees. I could, for instance, beat the trees with a baseball bat. Folk wisdom holds that a good beating gets the idea across to the trees. Then again, I could weigh down the branches to expose more of the tree to light and enhance fruiting. But these measures seem an intrusion upon the tree's natural growth and habits. Forcing the tree to yield to my will hasn't appealed to me. I don't rely on pears for my income. So I've learned to wait patiently for the trees to come around.

To everything there truly is a season. Fruit growing, especially, teaches me that. It's possible to rush the strawberry season and buy the berries in December and January, but the buyer pays a high price for low quality. In season, he pays a low price for high quality. It therefore pays to wait, and while waiting, forget any craving for the fruit that arises in the off seasons.

I'm finding that this approach is a good way to handle desire in any aspect of life. Not long ago, an acquaintance revealed that she'd been fantasizing about experiencing some new variations in her sex life, but that her upbringing was making her feel guilty. Her thoughts stoked the smoky furnaces of desire, yet she was afraid to act them out. The harder she struggled against the desires, the stronger they got.

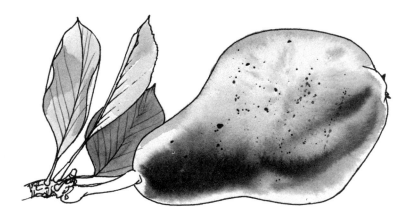

What if, I asked her, you could simply plant the seed of your desire in the cosmos, then wait patiently, find other things to do, and let go of the desire? What if you could trust the universe to know when and if the opportunity to fulfill the dream should present itself? What if you agree to be open to new experience, but not seek it out? The seeking, forcing, and bending of life to our personal desires often ruins the experience. One keeps the whole process clean by frankly admitting the desire, then expecting nothing. If the opportunity ever arises, one can choose on the spot whether or not to make the dream a reality. The experience comes at its own time, when it's ripe and right, and is, like the first pears from my Bartletts will undoubtedly be, a real gift.

Black
Walnut

*O*ne of the chief features of this place when we moved here was a 75-foot black walnut tree with a trunk 20 inches thick.

Placed three steps away from the corner of the front porch, it arched up and over the south end of the house.

We loved that tree. We strung a hammock beneath it, and Marilyn remembers lying in it on June afternoons, watching a mockingbird fly around in the gentle cage of the tree's green interior, listening to the bird's roll calls.

The nuts were unusual. Ordinary black walnuts have a shell as hard as Bakelite, with many small cul-de-sacs in which the nutmeat is enfolded. Getting the nutmeat out is difficult because the pieces are hard to get to, the shell is hard to crack, and pieces of broken shell are approximately the color of the nutmeat. A good chomp on a piece of shell can break a tooth.

Our tree's nuts, however, had a slightly thinner shell, and the nutmeat cavities were shallower. We often broke out whole quarters, and sometimes halves. A hickory tree nearby has nuts with the same good cracking qualities as the black walnut. I suppose both of them were selected strains—probably locally selected by the farm families who've lived here for hundreds of years.

Walnut shells come from the tree covered with a thick rind and a pebbley, yellowish green skin. The rind has to be removed before the nut can be cracked. When walnuts are ripening on the tree, the rind is white and clings tenaciously to the nut inside. After they finish ripening, they detach and fall. The white rind slowly turns to a slimy black goo that will stain everything it touches, especially human skin. Commercial black walnut stain is made from the gooey rinds. A tincture of black walnut rind was used at one time to cure ringworm. It's pungent, potent stuff, and it creates an impossible mess if you try to get it off the nuts.

What to do? Flip the fallen nuts into the driveway wheel tracks, and drive over them. The wheels smash them into a flat mass from which the nuts protrude like berries in a soup. I've learned to leave them alone for a couple of weeks. Rubber tires won't break the nuts, and rains will leach most of the black stain from the decaying walnut rind. I can then go along and pry the nuts out of the mass. They're relatively clean, and after a hosing and a few weeks of curing in the sun, they are ready to crack and enjoy.

We were very happy to have such a walnut tree by our house. But happiness often falls prey to destiny. One day about five years ago, we left the house to go shopping on a day hung with threatening clouds. On the way home the wind blew and pelting rain drove down. Lightning flashed. The wind picked up, bending big trees, and we pulled the car to the side of the road until the weather front passed.

When we got home, we saw at once the gaping hole in the sky where the walnut had been. Every one of its huge arms had snapped off and come crashing down. But not one had even touched the house, although the tree had grown over part of it. I later figured that if the limbs had fallen in almost any other configuration, one would surely have come straight through the roof, if not the skylight.

We were heartsick, of course. With chain saws we soon had the limbs cut and stacked for firewood, and the shattered trunk was cut off to the good wood, leaving a stump 18 feet high. There, where our magnificent walnut had been, was a huge, gaunt stump.

I've seen many growing plants regenerate themselves when cut back severely. I thought maybe the walnut stump would do the same thing. We argued the merits of cutting down the stump or seeing if it would grow again, deciding finally to give it a chance.

Today it's looking good. New limbs sprouted from the stump the next year. The mass of branches and leaves now makes a compact ball on the big trunk, as if a horticultural Paul Bunyan had been at work. It gets prettier every year. This year, for the first time since the tree blew down, it's carrying nuts.

According to the local Pennsylvania Dutch folklore, black walnuts were planted to protect the house from lightning. The shattered tree must have taken a big bolt. It worked, and it's growing skyward to work again.

Red
Raspberries

*M*y red raspberries were a gift from a woman who found me peering over her back fence. I'd been wandering the alleys of Allentown, checking out the backyard gardens while I waited for a dentist appointment. A large, healthy-looking stand of raspberries, dripping with bright red fruit, stopped me. I was admiring them when the lady of the house came out to see what I wanted.

We talked about raspberries for a while and she told me the strain she grew was given to her by someone whose husband travelled around the world for his company. She didn't know exactly where they were from, but they were supposed to be a superior variety. She offered me a clump, which I gladly took along.

At home the raspberries acted like they owned the place, throwing out underground roots in all directions. The next spring, canes started coming up everywhere within 5 feet of the original beds. The raspberry bed is now edged with railroad ties, and the few runners that make it under the ties and out on the other side are easily pulled when they send up canes.

To keep the berry bed to the size I want, I cut off most of the canes at ground level before they leaf out in the spring, leaving maybe two dozen canes that are trimmed back to 3 or 4 feet tall. These canes leaf out early and produce an early summer crop of berries—not a heavy crop, but with a good taste. The underground roots, meanwhile, are growing new canes that will fruit in late September and early October.

Thus, each spring I'm confronted with a jumble of dormant canes, some that grew the previous summer, and some, now two years old, that had borne the early summer fruit. All the two-year-old canes, along with most of the previous summer's canes, are cut down. The two dozen that I leave are one-year-old canes of superior appearance.

To someone like me, who grew up on the luscious, tart juiciness of wild wineberries—a close relative of the cultivated red raspberry—the taste of ripe red raspberries can be disappointing. They never taste quite as good as they look. I've found over the seasons that they taste best after they've hung in the cool fall air until just past dead ripe.

The wineberries grow all around the edges of my property, as if mocking the attempts of the cultivated berries to mimic their free, wild taste. Wineberries are an import from China, brought to America in the eighteenth century to be used in raspberry culture. Like my cultivated berries, they immediately struck out on their own, and today wineberries are common all over the eastern U.S.

There is an actual wild red raspberry, too. Some bushes grow on the top of our ridge. The berries are a little duskier than cultivated kinds, a little flatter, and taste awful. You can see the raspberry clan's ties to the rose family in the wild raspberry. The flowers that precede the berries are a light rosy pink, looking very much like the wild rose itself. In fact, raspberries and brambles are herbaceous examples and roses are woody examples of the family's traits.

Wineberries and wild red raspberries much prefer an eastern exposure, especially one in partial shade. You can find blackberries facing south, but rarely the wild red berries.

They appear near the edges of fields and along forest borders. The brambles figure centrally in the dramatic process of regeneration that Nature uses to reclothe her land after it is scarred. I realize now why red raspberries have such rooting strength. Their job is to colonize that bare soil as quickly as possible. The berries, among their other functions, are sure to attract both animals and birds and cause the patch to spread farther if more bare soil is nearby. But perhaps more importantly, the berries may also cause animals and birds to hang out at the berry patch, improving the soil with their droppings. Even the berries themselves, if they drop to the ground, will spill their sugar into the soil, where it will cause a healthy bloom of soil microorganisms. Nature does her utmost to get a little life going in turned-over soil, and the brambles are a part of that plan. Their shade also gives young trees and shrubs a start. Within not too many years, if left alone, a succession of different plants will follow the brambles until a climax forest returns.

America is called "the melting pot." I apply the term to plants as well as people. Right here on my hilltop there's a horticultural soup brewing just from red kinds of raspberries. How satisfying that the races of raspberries can share this land without warring against one another. Up close, each has a separate identity. From a distance, they merge with the rest of nature's vegetative manifestations to express the green thought that clothes the world.

Portulaca

I first encountered portulaca along a walk behind the Bee Lady's house. The Bee Lady ran a little business selling honey from the thirty-six hives her husband maintained, and spoke in a busy buzz as she made her transactions. To tell the truth, she acted very much like a bee, and resembled one too, with her pointed nose and horn-rimmed glasses.

Standing outside her back door, waiting for a 5-pound jar of wild-flower honey, I noticed a low growing plant with brilliant party-colored flowers edging the concrete walk. Roselike blossoms covered succulent stems that grew in mats only 6 inches high. Each plant carried flowers of a different color and each color came in varying shades. I saw yellows, oranges, reds, pinks, lavenders, magentas, white, and cream. They were candy colors, cartoon colors, all of them cheerful and bold.

The Bee Lady said the plants were portulaca. She told me how she first planted it there several years before as an annual, and that it reseeded itself, reappearing every year along the sunny edge of the walk.

With its bright and varied colors and profuse flowers, portulaca seemed like a perfect welcome for any passing bee. All of a piece with the Bee Lady and her honey-stocked house.

We've long since brought portulaca home to our own garden. We first tried to establish it in our lower flower garden, hoping it would reseed itself each year as it had at the Bee Lady's. In subsequent years a few plants came up, but only a few, and finally the portulaca disappeared.

Then last season we finished off the centerpiece of the vegetable garden—a raised square of soil, 12 feet on a side, bordered by railroad ties, with a large triangular rock in the center. This past spring Marilyn planted the square with portulaca, and over the summer it has filled the area right up to the railroad ties. Now the rock floats serenely in a prismatic pool of day-glow colors.

Not far from the portulaca is a long row of culinary thyme that's irresistible to bees. During its blooming period from mid-June through July, each small, bushy plant carries a sprinkling of honeybees tumbling over its myriad tiny lavender flowers, fumbling to get the microscopic droplets of strongly scented nectar.

We didn't realize it at planting time, but the center of our garden, seen from above by a bee, must be the most luscious invitation imaginable.

The Bee Lady and her husband, old when we knew them, died over a decade ago, and now their house is gone to strangers who don't seem to care about flowers and bees. The hives were long ago sold off, and the land has returned to half-grown trees and brush, far less hospitable to bees than the meadows of wild flowers and fields of buckwheat that were once set out for their delectation.

Our patch of portulaca serves as a memory of the Bee Lady. Her spirit is there, and as a consequence, so are the bees.

Black-Eyed Susan

*I*n August, both field and garden in our part of the world clothe themselves in the richest gold, reflecting the burnished light falling from the late summer sun. Along the roadsides and in dense stands in old fields, *Rudbeckia hirta* opens. These wild Black-Eyed Susans keep company with blue chicory and red clover by the asphalt roads that crisscross our hills. Seen from the window of a passing car, the gold, blue, and red dots of these flowers merge into a variegated tapestry slipping past the edges of vision.

In our garden, *Rudbeckia fulgida* 'Goldsturm' slathers its deep golden butter across the tops of the beds. It strikes the keynote color, the one from which the other colors of August are derived. Its intense gold is refined in the nearby *Achillea filipendulina* 'Coronation Gold.' A further attenuation of the rudbeckia's color yields the bright yellow of *Coreopis verticillata* on the other side of the bed. Farther away, the yellow becomes paler in a clump of lemon yellow daylilies, and finally it barely colors the petals of a single daylily by the garden steps.

Protruding into the middle of this gold and yellow garden, tiger lilies have hung out their recurved, polka-dotted flowers. The lilies are a fleshy reddish orange, toned down to a waxy shade. Their petals are speckled with dots of the same black-brown as the centers of the black-eyed Susans. Even so, the gold rudbeckias and the orange lilies clash.

The clash is not dramatic, as with complementary colors, but dull, sickening, like an afternoon spent in a badly decorated room watching reruns on T.V.

Some color clashes, especially violent ones, can be used to add some . . . well, violence to an otherwise dull corner of the garden.

But this clash seems unredeemable. Try as I might, I can't bring the deep gold and waxy orange into a harmony. I've looked at the flowers from several angles, hoping to find a way to understand a unity between them, a suggestion of a shared meaning. But all I've gotten is the same old reaction: yuck.

Apart from each other, in association with other flowers, each color is legitimate and beautiful. The lilies go well with reddish *Phlox paniculata*, and the black-eyed Susans go with all the blue, yellow, and red flowers.

I thought yesterday about moving the lilies out of the way, closer to the phlox and out of the line of sight from the front porch to the rudbeckias.

This morning, in one last stab at reconciliation, I plucked a fresh lily blossom and a large rudbeckia flower and brought them in the house. They sit before me now, their petals intertwined. And here, against the wooden simplicity of the kitchen table, I see at last their secret harmony.

Here the yellow and orange are natural allies with the dark brown oak table top. The black eye of the Susan, the speckles on the lily and its six dark stamens, are deepened shades of old wood. The flesh-colored lily pistil is capped with a velvet tuft of deep red oxblood. The orange, red, brown, and gold of these flowers now sing together, with the slightest note of dissonance carried by a bright green sheath at the lily pistil's base.

The shimmering greens that dominate the garden are the culprit, after all. Black-eyed Susans and tiger lilies are the best of friends against a brown or neutral background, but in the garden, green forces them into a mutual antagonism.

And yet, in the garden is where they must live. The answer is to move the lilies, and from time to time bring cut flowers from both plants into the house for a truce, for a communion of antagonists.

So it would be, I believe, with any antagonists if they could be removed from their context. The Russian and the American meeting, perhaps, in Rome, where against an Italian background they could find each other's humanity. The family members whose long-standing resentments prevent their speaking at home, meeting by chance in a place like Singapore, where what they have in common would stand out in bold relief against the unfamiliar culture.

These August flowers reveal to me that disputes are usually contextual, and that resolving them can be as simple as changing a point of view.

Catnip

*O*ur cats usually reserve a little dignity when they play tricks on one another and perform their stunts. But dignity evaporates when they hit our patch of catnip. Their eyes glaze over. They roll and loll on the plants, then sit bolt upright with a crazy, unfocused gleam in their eyes. They dart around, taking the odd swipe at nothing. Then they wobble away and sit somewhere until they come to their senses.

Researchers have found that cats react in this strange, comical way to a volatile oil produced by the plant to keep insects away. Spearmint and peppermint are cousins of catnip that have a milder oil: The mints only refresh us; they don't make us cavort about like a nipped cat.

It makes me wonder about the effects plants in general have on humans. Some plants produce deadly poisons, able to snuff us out like candles in a windstorm. The intense poison in the destroying angel mushroom, *Amanita verna*, is so toxic to humans, one suspects it's made for us.

Then there are the slow poisons, like the absinthe in wormwood that shattered the health of several generations of Bohemian Parisians.

The psychotropic and physiologic properties of plants puzzle me. Why would *Cannabis sativa* produce a substance that alters human consciousness? Why should the herb valerian produce compounds that calm a hyperactive mind? Or foxglove secrete substances that can regulate our heartbeat?

One plant, like a potato, is nutritious and can help build a strong human frame; another, like jimson weed, can tear apart a human mind.

The answer, I think, lies in the interrelatedness of all flesh, both red and green. There could be no animals without plants. Through the eons of co-evolution, plants have gained the ability to affect animals. In their ceaseless production of compounds that modify animal behavior, plants were bound to create some unintended and even silly effects on nontarget animals.

We need look no farther than the catnip. Its botanical name, *Nepeta cataria*, refers to its strange effect on cats. And, in fact, the word catnip means "cat's nep," the last word a shortening of nepeta, or mint. The plant is sometimes called catmint.

Surely the effect on cats is an unintended side effect of the plant's defense mechanism against herbivorous insects. But if I have a sense of humor, why should the rest of creation lack it? I like to think that the catnip fills an evolutionary niche requiring the existence of a substance that makes cats silly. Otherwise the innate dignity of cats would be insufferable arrogance. Pride goeth before a pratfall.

Nature has evolved the cat, and to the delight of us all, man and cat, has also dreamed up a plant that plays them a gentle joke.

Figs

*F*or the past three years I've gone to the garden in November to dig out the fig tree. I take up a root ball the size of the galvanized washtub in which the tree will spend the winter. Prying it loose with the spading fork breaks off all the long, searching roots that have grown far into the garden soil over the season.

In its native habitat, my shrubby little fig would be a huge tree. Here in Pennsylvania, where winter temperatures can be 45 degrees colder than a fig tree can stand, digging it out each fall keeps the roots pruned and the topgrowth to 4 feet high and 4 feet across.

On moving day, after the fig drops its leaves, I bring a wheelbarrow and washtub to the garden. When the root ball comes loose, I hoist it into the washtub, add soil from the hole until the fig is potted up in the tub, and wheel it to the house. I have then to wrestle the tub out of the wheelbarrow and down to the bottom cellar step. And there the fig tree stays, dormant, needing only a few waterings, until about the first of May.

The first time I did this, I worried about the fig. Would it survive with severed roots in the dark, cold cellar? Would the tree leaf out too early if the cellar warmed up too fast in the spring? Would I forget to water it enough? Would the roots die out and kill it?

I needn't have worried. The tree wintered over perfectly and leafed out as soon as it was replanted in the garden. The fig went to sleep in the garden and it woke up in the garden, albeit with severely pruned roots.

Last year in July it sprouted its first crop of little green figs. About a dozen of them appeared at various places along the branches. At the time, I guessed that they'd never have time to ripen, that too few days remained in the growing season. Sure enough, cold nights and shortening days sent the plant to sleep long before the figs grew to size.

Here was a new worry—for if the plant always set out fruit in July, then I'd never eat its figs.

Again, I needn't have worried. This past spring, just before I put the tree back in the garden, it popped out a half dozen fruits. Now it's late July and these early figs are well on their way to ripening—I estimate they'll be ready to pick by September. The tree put out another crop of figs this week, but they won't ripen before frost.

Today, as I looked at the figs ripening on their branches, I saw that they sprang from random places, like warts on the back of your thumb. I remembered my worries about the plant and called myself a worrywart.

I was afraid the plant would die. I was afraid it wouldn't ripen any figs. I was anxious, not about real problems, but about unreal problems that I'd created out of ignorance.

What other unreal problems demanded that I pay them attention, I wondered. Several worries hung on my mind. They seemed real enough to give my stomach a queasy feeling when I thought about them. But in truth, nothing I worried about had come to pass. Perhaps nothing would. Away with my perfervid mind's phantasms!

I found myself centered in the moment, in a sunny garden with my ripening figs. Everything was okay. Trouble would have to wait until trouble actually appeared.

When the mind is full of self-created fear, the body reacts with anxious stress, a form of negative self-absorption that chews on itself. A sunny outlook dispels the darkness and the worries that grow in it. For positive reassurance of this truth, I need only look at my fat figs.

Watermelon

On my tenth birthday, one of my presents was a packet of watermelon seeds. Compared to the other games and goodies, it hardly rated a second notice that day.

About a week later I finally got around to inspecting the packet. Soon I was in my parent's garden, spading up five hills in the pattern of a five of spades. Five seeds went into each hill. Later my father showed me how to thin the plants to the strongest looking seedling. Under his encouragement I watered them through dry spells and watched in growing amazement as my little seedlings quietly, and with an ever-increasing vigor, took over the garden. My mom's flowers, the peppers, all went down under the floodtide of watermelon vines.

Then the flood crested and the vines subsided in the weakening light of August, revealing the huge green barrels of the melons littered across the ground.

I was only a kid, yet the melons had come through for me. It worked! Watermelon, I saw, was a very impressive and powerful plant, and the sight of its harvest of sweet melons thrilled me.

If I remember right, there were six or eight big melons, but my dad said they weren't ripe, and he'd thump their sides as if that were proof.

I tested the first melon by cutting out a long, wedge-shaped slice of pinkish white flesh that was neither sweet nor ripe. I reinserted the wedge, figuring that no harm had been done. A few days later, having convinced myself that the melons must surely be ripe, I cut a melon free and carried it down the hill to a cold, spring-fed creek to cool it over-

night. The next morning I broke it open to find a promising, but unripe, interior. That melon was broken against a tree.

Again I waited for a few days, feeling patient at first but becoming increasingly restless with each walk out to the melon patch. I wouldn't want them to get too ripe. So I took a wedge again, this time from a third unripe melon.

By the time the melons did get ripe, there was only one sound specimen left. All the others had slices where I'd tested them, and the fruit rotted before it ripened.

Since then, I've spoiled many a melon by picking it too early. But this year is different. I'm going to wait. Self-control will be my middle name. I'll wait until the traditional thump yields a hollow thud. Until the white spot underneath turns a yellowish white. Until the stem starts to dry. Until the curling tendrils on either side of the stem turn brown.

I see now that my first garden taught me patience: one of the great lessons a garden can impart to an open soul, and one of the most difficult. I haven't forgotten it, even if I don't practice it perfectly.

In fact, I could go for some watermelon right now. And there is a nice one up in the patch.

The only real improvement in my behavior since that first garden is that now I thump and observe instead of hacking up the melons with a knife. They are still intolerably slow to ripen.

Japanese
Maple

Our dwarf Japanese maple perches serenely above several large slabs of limestone that are entirely encrusted in large, white, terminated quartz crystals. The deeply cleft leaves drape their delicate filigree over the rocks, obscuring the hard boundaries where white crystals meet brown mulch. Red leaves and white crystals merge. Beneath the little tree and the quartz slabs, a pool of smaller, loose crystals gathers beside the blue-green crinkled leaves of *Hosta tokudama*, another Japanese horticultural development.

On the ground under the Japanese maple, a mat of *Mazus reptans* creeps away toward the path behind the garden. In the spring, this mat is covered profusely with small blue and white flowers that consort with the maple's red leaves.

The tree is very dwarf and resembles a bonsai both when it's in leaf and during the winter. In color, form, and function in the garden, the tree is exquisite. I can't think of a more beautiful member of the plant kingdom among the hundreds of species that grow here.

I sat on a large rock not far from the tree the other day and wondered what makes this particular plant so beautiful. What is the strange attraction that calls from the things we find beautiful and turns our affection toward them? We love beautiful people and things, sometimes despite ourselves, sometimes with a heart freely given.

A peculiarly deep pain sears the heart when a person we find beautiful spurns our affection. Because our hearts are opened by their beauty, rejection cuts to the core, challenging our sense of self-worth, leaving us feeling worthless and ugly. Lucky is the person whose love is requited.

Beauty of any kind, physical or otherwise, sings a siren song to the heart. The heart will always respond with love, and often with a desire to somehow possess the beauty. It's the desire that causes the trouble. Love much and desire little, if you would enjoy the world's beauty to the fullest.

These were my thoughts as I studied the Japanese maple. My affection and appreciation were neither rejected nor requited. With beautiful plants, they don't have to be. That their beauty can touch our hearts is fulfillment enough.

My maple tree is beautiful partly because it's in the right place, adding its grace notes to a composed landscape, adding red to green, setting off the large leaves of the hostas with its fine, lacy foliage. The tree is also inherently beautiful because of its unique shape and form.

But none of this gets to the essence of its beauty, or why it should strike my heart. At the core, beauty is inseparable from love. It happens within us, though we find it outside ourselves. It's the universal affinity that binds the world together, and the closest we get to truth in this world.

Rose

*A*n old-fashioned, single-petalled rose grew by the side of our house when we moved to this property.

There's not much to it. Just a few canes emerge from the old root each year. The flowers appear sparsely. Compared to most roses, they're inconspicuous: just an inch or so across; light pink with yellow stamens clustering around a white pistil in the center; slightly, sweetly fragrant; dependable.

Over the years, we've tried many varieties of commercial roses. Last year we planted *Rosa rubrifolia,* a vigorous species rose whose chief beauty is the reddish blue foliage and orange hips that create a color sensation in the fall. We also put in White Dawn, a climber, by the arbor in the upper garden. Two years later, it has yet to reach the top.

Another climber, Don Juan, once resided by the upper garden path. Our idea was to train it to grow up and over an arching pergola, creating a stunning entrance to the garden proper. Don Juan puts forth big, dark red, heavily scented flowers, perfect announcements for the perennial borders beyond.

But Don Juan, for some still unfathomable reason, drooped, curled under, and died in its second season. So did the *Rosa rugosa* that we put by the red currant bushes. Here the idea was to have red currants early and *R. rugosa*'s large, edible fruits late.

White Dawn and *Rosa rubrifolia* may last; they may not. Rose culture, we've found, requires a lot of attention, more than we've been willing to give. We don't like to spray, and that has allowed the fungi, bacteria, Japanese beetles, and rose chafers to take their tolls.

And yet, we don't lack for roses. The little old-fashioned rose blooms modestly by the house each year, and within the jumble of shrubs along our fence rows, the small pink blossoms of wild multiflora roses open regularly.

Last winter I chanced across a poem that asked me if I knew "the secret shut within the bosom of the rose." It's to these uncultivated species that I go when I want an answer from a rose.

This year I found three small pink buds on a wild rosebush in a nearby field, brought them home, and ensconced them in a small vase. I watched closely day by day, waiting for them to open, suspecting they'd spill their secret when they did.

One morning when I came downstairs to put on a pot of coffee, three opened blossoms greeted me. The petals had unfurled just enough to form deep cups, three whirlpools of pink silk, each holding a golden bouquet of stamens. From close up, they wafted a scent like the pure note of a coloratura. Perfect little roses.

By lunchtime the petals had unfurled too far and the flowers were flat and full-blown. By dinnertime, they were past full bloom. The next day, they were ready for the compost bin. With hindsight, I thought I saw their secret: Beauty peaks for only a moment, then fades. No sooner does an eclipse begin than it's over. The moment that summer begins is the same moment that the sun starts its journey south.

But there was more enfolded within the bosom of the rose. If I thought of the rose in its entirety, first as a young bud, then a red bud, then a perfect rose, then a faded flower, and finally as a fruit, I could see that its moment of perfection is entirely predicated on its other moments. Without the bud, there will be no perfect rose. Without the faded flower, there could have been no perfect rose.

All moments, then, share in the perfect moment, and if we could but see it clearly, all moments are perfect.

Epilogue

*T*he writing of this book has revealed to me that Marilyn and I have accomplished our dream here. These five acres, bordered by woods and fields beyond, lie tucked away out of sight of any road. We created what's here from raw materials and imported plants. In the end, after twelve years, it has been realized. All the potential we felt when we moved here has been actualized. The garden's beauty is due more to nature's ability to work with our suggestions than to our enforcement of a preconceived idea. It truly is finished as far as we're concerned, as this past growing season proved.

From beginning to end, fresh flowers burst out exuberantly everywhere—sometimes from roots we'd planted, sometimes from nature's volunteers—in such profusion as I've never seen before. The fruit trees all gave generously—some for the first time. The tomato plants showered us with fruit. The watermelons grew fat in the patch. As I wrote my way around the property, each plant seemed to dress itself up with a vigor and shine that was new to me. Usually, the vagaries of the weather favor some plants and displease others—it's too dry for the forget-me-nots, it's too wet for the yarrow. But this year, every plant on the place found the weather to its liking and flourished. Even the local farmers are

210

remarking about the way the dry weather holds after mowing hay, and how the rains have come generously at proper intervals, how there've been no gales
to blow down wheat and corn, and no hail to shoot
holes in the grape leaves.

After years of struggling against thistle and
briar, I've hardly seen a one this year. I think I've
won the battle, if not the war. The sumac is finally
out of the field and the Jerusalem artichokes have
been beaten back into prescribed areas. Even the
crabgrass has been manageable.

Little bonuses have followed our footsteps this
year. The strawberries returned from a year off and
gave us sweetness we didn't expect. After five empty
seasons, the wren house on our porch is occupied
with cheeping chicks and busy parents. We discovered a patch of lunaria behind the toolshed that
must have self-sown from a plant we put there years
ago and had forgotten about. Bright magenta silene
appeared everywhere from seed scattered by wind
from a few plants the year before. Bachelor's buttons did the same thing, filling in with true blue to
tone down the loud note of the silene.

Our early expectations here were modest and
the reality of our achievements has far exceeded
them. We were overwhelmed more than once by the
brilliance of the garden's display. In early June,
Marilyn ran to me across the lawn, laughing and
crying at the same time. "It's so beautiful," she said.

That's when we knew it was finished. The can-
vas was complete. It was time to start anew some-
place else. As I write this in the waning days of

August, the house is packed into numbered boxes
that sit all around me. Within a few days, we'll all be
in California. We chose Sonoma County, about as far
north of San Francisco as this place is north of Philadelphia, for many reasons, not least among them the
fact that Luther Burbank chose Sonoma County as
the place to do his major research in the early years
of this century. If it was good enough for Luther, it's
good enough for us.

We'll start a new place. All that we've made
actual here will revert to potential there. We'll learn
a new climate, new plants, new ideas. It's exciting
and rejuvenating.

But here, now, are the last few days I'll ever
spend on my Pennsylvania hilltop, and the feeling is
poignant. So much of Marilyn and me is in this place.
Our psychic roots are deep, and digging them up and
moving them across the continent will be, I'm sure,
as hard on us at first as transplanting a favored
flower. But perhaps we'll be like the daylilies and
hardly notice that we've moved.

We see that the great display this year meant
goodbye. I also see that this book is my goodbye to
the plants I've included, and to those I haven't. Although personal, I believe that these essays apply to
all of us who love our plants and hear their silent
suggestions.

California represents a new start for us. There
will be new and better gardens. We have everything
to learn about gardening there. Learning is the essence of growth, and growth is the essence of life.
That's the main thing I'll take with me as I leave
these gardens behind.